# HARVEST
### of LIGHT

# HARVEST of LIGHT

**An Artist's Journey**
STEPHANIE QUAINTON STEEL

Orca Book Publishers

First edition.

**Canadian Cataloguing in Publication Data**
Steel, Stephanie Quainton, 1935 —
   Harvest of light

ISBN  0-920501-64-8

1. Steel, Stephanie Quainton, 1935 — Journeys — British Columbia — Pacific Coast.  2. Pacific Coast (B.C.) — Description and travel.  I. Title.
ND249.S73A2 1991    917.1104'4    C91-091540-7


Publication assistance provided by the Canada Council


Cover design by Susan Fergusson
Cover paintings by the author
Printed and bound in Canada


**Orca Book Publishers**
**P.O. Box 5626, Station B**
**Victoria, B.C., Canada  V8R 6S4**

IN MEMORY of my father, Eric Hugh Quainton, and to all those who care about the fragile future of the B.C. wilderness.

# Contents

# 1.   Floating World

ON MY dresser is a photograph. It is faded and yellowed with time, but the figure stands clear, a tall Victorian lady in a long skirt. She has left behind sixteen servants in China who once did all the cooking and tending for a family of seven. She stands preparing a meal on a small woodstove that is set up on rocks at the edge of a forest on the banks of the sea. My mother's mother is the lady working this open-air kitchen. The year is 1919. The Hinton family is looking for a summer property near the end of the Interurban Railroad in Deep Cove, Vancouver Island.

That summer of the photograph, the family rented a camping spot among the trees on a farm at the foot of Downey Road. They pitched their tents between the rows of hops and asparagus. While my grandmother cooked the evening meal, the trees absorbed the smoke and wafted it seaward, lending a misty atmosphere to the scene. Grandpa took one more photo, caught one more clue of the new life they were living in Canada.

Threading through the genes of my forebears on both sides of the family were certain signals. I was an offshoot of the photograph, a part of my grandmother's ability to adapt to circumstance, and a part of my grandfather's leaning toward art, and my story begins in Deep Cove.

The family waited that summer for a suitable property to come on the market. When the chance came to buy the piece of waterfront adjacent to their camping spot, which held a commercial boat-building establishment on it, my grandparents took action. What better summer residence for their sizable family than a large boathouse in Deep Cove?

During the first winter on the new property, my grandfather and a friend went to work framing in a ten-foot porch around the entire circumference of the building. They also added a second storey with eight bedrooms that were made accessible from the top bank by the installation of two long, thick planks for travel back and forth to a privy outside.

In later years the offspring of my grandparents and their children descended on the boathouse in the summertime to enjoy a busy social life. The bedrooms would be filled to capacity, and tents would be pitched on the beach and the bank to accommodate the numerous family members.

Eight beds squeaked on old soft woven wire bedsprings. I would hear bats outside at night and the swallows nesting in the eaves, but the sound of lapping waves from the sea underneath sang louder to me, and sweeter, as at high tide it permeated the cracks in the old wooden structure. In spite of a fear of water, I was lured toward the ocean.

The fear was not unnatural. Taken out to swim on my mother's back, I would fight and scream. Forced to cross the bay to family picnics, I was alarmed by the tipping and bobbing of the boat, which seemed entirely at the mercy of the waves as the ocean floor receded into a deep green murky unknown. I can still remember throwing myself down onto the deck of the family lifeboat, to lie amongst the feet of family members, my head only inches from another horror, cold pea salad.

But my early fears changed, and the change was motivated by jealousy of my older sister, who was taken fishing by my grandfather. She came back parading her prize, a twelve-inch grilse. My grandfather slit the gleaming trophy in half lengthwise and gave Dalla a lesson from start to finish on how to clean, debone, cook and at last eat her trophy.

Seeing the look of envy on my face, my perceptive

grandfather in a quiet moment alone with me asked if I, too, would like to try fishing with him. "But only if the water's calm," he said, with much insight.

I watched the weather all the next day. When silence in the boathouse indicated that my grandfather had finished his cello practice, I knew it was time. We set out with no one but us on the beach; he saw to that. I took his hand, stepped over the gunwales and sat down in the stern. I kept my eyes inside the boat, as it moved and took on a life of its own. I kept my eyes on my grandfather.

Grandfather went through the entire performance with a knowing smile on his face. Later, he taught me to clean and debone, to cook and to eat what I had caught. I asked him when we could go again. I had overcome my first fears of the sea.

My grandfather had two boats, a fourteen-footer and a ten-footer, both of them lapstrake clinkers. I soon undertook rowing the boats myself. In my early teens I would rise at four in the loft of the boathouse to the sound of the tide lapping around the pylons underneath. I would hear my father, also an avid fisherman, dragging his clinker toward the water before it was light. Hurrying into clothes, I would tear down to the bank at the back to the smaller boat, just in time to solicit his help with the launching before he left shore. Off I'd row, careful not to head in the same direction as him. My father, showing the recognizable family independence, chose to be alone; that was why he loved fishing, he said. It was a way to escape the family hordes. "The sea is only just large enough for two boats," he would say, adding, "And then, only if they keep their distance." Secretly, he made sure he was never far away.

A hundred feet offshore I would unwind a green cotton handline, still damp from the day before. I'd bait the lure my grandfather had given me. Then I would tie the pulling end to a willow withe, jam it into the gunwales, and begin trolling. The stick would wiggle within a few moments on most mornings. That would mean a fish. There was no limit to what you caught, and a morning without a fish was rare.

Every so often my father would drift past. We would drop our oars to signal the size of any catch or shake our heads if there had been no action. Neither my father nor I had any desire to be onshore with crowds of people. Alone, the world of our boats suited us far better. I was learning that the floating world had much to offer.

One evening when I was lucky enough to have won by default the master bedroom, one of two that faced south out over the water, my father showed up in my room just before dark. "Here, take this line and when you see me come around in the boat, let the hook down to me. Then I want you to play out line until I tell you to stop." I saw my father row out

until he disappeared into the gathering dark, his voice finally coming back, "That's enough!"

Fifteen minutes went by. I heard him pull the boat back up to its resting place on the bank above the tide. He returned to my room. "There might just be a good-sized fish on that by morning," he said, as he tied the line to the headstead of my bed. "But it's my fish, so don't fool with the line."

I fell in love with my father and with the sea. Had my father's attention remained undeterred, and had the sea remained abundant with fish, I might have been happy with this existence for a lifetime, this childhood of catching fish on calm waters. But it was not to be . . .

Through the years I kept the photograph on my dresser. I was related, I thought, but not related to the two figures, the one visible as she tended her stove in the new world, the other not visible as he set up his tripod and prepared the camera.

It had not always been family life that Grandfather used to capture on film. He had once hidden on a roof at the gates to China's Forbidden City to photograph the dowager empress as she passed through the crowd. The Chinese punishment for daring even to look at her was instant decapitation. Heaven only knows what they would have done to an Englishman. While the villagers kowtowed, my grandfather lined up his shot.

My great grandmother had also exhibited a certain courage with life. During a typhoon while crossing the seas from England to China by sailing ship, she refused to go below, but chose staying on deck as the lesser of the evils. Even though one of her children had sickened and died during the long, arduous crossing, she preferred to meet her fate face on.

Her daughter, my grandmother, refused to leave the city of Tientsin when it was being shelled during the Boxer Rebellion. She nursed her first baby and hid below the floors, refusing to leave with the others who fled the town.

By comparison, my own life paled. I had never ventured far from shore. Staying in calm waters, I grew up, took a job in a Victoria bank. I was married, gave up the job to raise children, then was not married, and I came back to Deep Cove with my two daughters and settled near the old family home where I had spent childhood summers. Life would have been easy and predictable, but the photograph filled me with a restlessness to be doing something more exciting than just the mundane. I had no idea what it might be, but I kept the photograph visible. I saw it every morning as I rose and I wondered when the adventure would start.

At the prompting of a cousin I had begun to paint. When my first paintings were sold, all of them, in a community bazaar, I began to get more serious. There was the chance of a job in an art store and I took it, so that I could learn more about art products and so that I could pay the mortgage on my land in Deep Cove. I used the scarce leftover money to buy art supplies, and I managed to buy a boat, a clinker in great need of repair. I put it on the old family beach, which now belonged to my uncle. I lured my children out using the pretext of teaching them to fish at an early age, but my daughters had inherited the recognizable independent spirit. They said it was cruel to fish, and that they would rather be elsewhere, so I let them go off in the direction of their choice.

One day I took a sketchbook with me in the boat. I began to draw the things that drifted past, and the changing shoreline. As time went by there was a subtle change: I began to fish less and draw more; I took art supplies with me and often forgot the bait. And I began to like rowing for its own sake. I was attracted to the changing scenery more than the fish.

Each trip I made was pulling me a little further out into the landscape. I had become enchanted. I was to realize later that the people in the photograph had been innocent, too; it had all been circumstance.

# 2.   Boats

MY LIFE as an artist really began when I donated one of my paintings to a charity event. Shortly after the affair, I heard a rumour that a new gallery in Victoria had bought it. With my curiosity piqued, I went and found the painting for sale in a prominent place on the gallery's walls. I was asked to bring in more of my work on consignment. Four years of lessons from two of Victoria's leading artists were at last producing results. Why shouldn't I attempt to earn some of the investment back?

Boats, I was told, would be the most likely to sell. If I was to paint boats, then I would start my own boat fund, thought I. It was time to purchase a canoe and move further afield than just the waters of Deep Cove.

I called my canoe *Soulcatcher* after a Kwakiutl myth about a two-headed serpent that could keep a soul trapped in its middle. Names for my boats were important to me.

Those were halcyon days. I would take breakfast, lunch, or supper and, since neither of my two daughters seemed to share my wish to be waterborne, I put a rock in the bow instead of a partner and began to paddle a little further from home, on Beaver Lake, ten miles away. I would throw in a bag of pencils and sketchbooks and off I would go. I would paddle out to sit dreaming an artist dream and shading in

trees that burst with new leaf or faded to burnt sienna and let go of their leaves. It was an artist's heaven to drift in a boat on calm water.

One day the apparition of my tiny car with a large canoe on the roof attracted Frank Johnson, a pillar of the local canoe club. Frank suggested a membership. I told him the canoe was only a method to help me with art. He told me it was art enough just to learn to paddle a canoe, that a few basic lessons would increase my range of where I could go.

With my membership and new companions to paddle with, I ventured farther afield, into the waters of Brentwood Bay, Esquimalt Lagoon, and even Sidney when the weather and currents were calm enough. Most often I paddled with a group. But no one paused long enough to allow me to sketch, and for awhile my interest in art was all but forgotten as the excitement of new-found paddling skills became an end in itself. I saved the introspective trips with pen and paper for other times as I experienced the exhilaration of paddling face to the wind. I wanted to learn to go further, faster . . . for life had become an adventure.

On one canoe club outing the group was accompanied by a family in a fleet of solo boats, kayaks. A kayak had all the qualities for independence, I thought, as I noticed that, although the family paddled together, they powered their boats alone. Thoughts of trying to balance a sketchbook and wield a pen as I bobbed around came to mind, but I shoved them aside in a fervour for this new and independent method of travel. It was no longer enough to always manage the prow of the canoe and have a partner make all the decisions at the stern. I wanted to control my own craft.

It turned out that a club member had a second-hand kayak for sale, and it wasn't long before we made a deal at a price I could just afford. So my red canoe went to rest on sawhorses beside the clinker. Next to it, and nearest the car, I placed my mustard-coloured English estuary kayak. I called her *Loon*, after one of the most enchanting of seabirds.

*Loon*, unlike her namesake, was beamy with a low prow and stern. But she lacked a seat and I soon found that in waves higher than a foot, she shipped water over her deck. Because she tended to spear the waves in front of her, I often got dragged along, an unwilling passenger under control of the waves over the bow. "Are you planning to dive for pearls?" teased my boating friends. *Loon* had been cheap, in part because she lacked a seat. I built her one by gluing in a pad of closed-cell ethafoam and perched myself on top.

I had a lot to learn about kayaking. Without a seat, I just rolled around when the weather was rough. Then a kayaking member of the canoe club offered to teach me some of the basics. We took trips into rougher and rougher weather until I implored him to accompany me back to shore. I felt disgraced. My companion explained that an estuary kayak was

not shaped for the high waves and currents of open-water travel, that the missing seat just complicated the problem and that these things were good for me to know. He was right.

I returned to sulk in Deep Cove and on Elk Lake. But I soon began to miss the more open places as *Loon* and I continued our battle for supremacy even of the calm water. One day I was struggling to make shore in low beam seas just off Deep Cove. I braced against the vicious sidewind and was trying to remember what I could of Fred's teaching when a shadow passed through the edge of my vision. I looked up, startled. There passed not thirty feet from me a slender streamlined dart. I watched it sparkle in the sun. "Helloo," the paddler called out as he streaked by heading for some perfect target along the bay. The wind meant nothing to him or his boat. I stared after him, in awe of the kayaker's silent determination, the boat's swiftness, its perfect design.

As soon as I returned to the beach, I rushed into Victoria to the local canoe base to ask my friend, Derek, to identify the craft. "It would be a Nordkapp," he said without hesitation, and went for his catalogues. "Six of these boats have just completed an expedition around Cape Horn," he said as he rummaged through his file.

Then she must be the craft for me, I thought, under my breath.

As Derek's stories of the Nordkapp unfurled, I began to see a rainbow of possibilities. I saw myself a centaur of the sea, half human, half kayak, covering the world's oceans, laughing in the wind. I blinked at the vision, remembered my grandparents and their courage. The scene grew until I, too, was taking on the Horn in a bath of blowing wavetops.

"A Nordkapp can take you where any dream of sketching calls," said Derek with finality as he got out his order book.

My heart was beating fast. I quickly had to explain that although my desire was large, my purse was small.

I went home despondent. I had just given up my art store job. Would the new gallery give me an exhibition? So far, sales of my paintings were in no hurry to make me rich. My heart went on longing for possession. The memory of the Nordkapp that had passed me in the bay would not leave my dreams. I went to the local harbours and frantically worked on more paintings of boats. I had a desperate wish to make money quickly. I knew that at the end of it, when I could order the English Nordkapp, I would have access to the real floating world, the one that now lay just beyond reach, trying to entice me to be honest with my art, but that would have to wait while I did my harbour paintings. Courage, said my inner self. Think of the photograph — it took the family a long time to reach the shores of Canada.

# 3.  Omens

BOATS ARE a world unto themselves, I thought, as I perched my new yellow kayak on the shore at Esquimalt Lagoon. She had not a scratch or blemish upon her sleek fibreglass hull that morning as I pointed her bow toward the small waves that slipped up the sand in twelve-foot swaths. It was a calm day in November. Standing beside her, I wiggled into the rubber spraydeck, and, holding my paddle across the afterdeck to form a balance like an outrigger, I eased myself into the cockpit and slipped the hem of the rubber skirt over the coaming.

Buying the Nordkapp had cost me a year of my savings and a year learning kayak safety in the local swimming pool. Launching had become a familiar drill. I held the paddle upright with the blade touching the shore. With paddle and hand I would turtle-walk seawards. Timing was essential; I must observe the waves and pick a rising one to launch quickly while it was at its maximum height. If I didn't I could be slapped back to shore sideways, losing all momentum and my dignity to boot. The Nordkapp was a tippy boat, yet I had every faith in her sense of balance. If I were to spill, it would be the fault of the paddler and not the boat.

I was seaborne. Paddling hard, I broke through the waves before they tumbled and smashed along the shore. I turned to paddle along just beyond the surfline, parallel to the beach. Ahead of me lay the old barge-loading ramp at the Colwood gravel pit. My mind returned instantly to childhood, to the place where my sister and I had dared one another to climb onto the loaded conveyer belt that carried the gravel along the wharf to be dumped onto a barge. There was a twenty-foot drop to the shore below. If we didn't get off in time, there was the threat of being carried to the stone sort to be graded to size.

Being the younger sister, I had leapt off with adrenalin surging the moment I got on, to sit on the safe bank and watch my sister as she rode the belt like it was a charger, arms flung free, until she was out in space. She would hurl herself back at the last possible moment. In the pressure of competition I learned early that my fears could drive me from succeeding. I looked at the silent shoreline in the November quiet. The conveyer belt was nowhere in sight. I had never ridden it out from the bank.

Paddling along the shoreline, I saw the mounds of sand and gravel that recalled another of our childhood games. On the plateau immediately above the pit was the local rifle club's skeet field. The clatter of shotgun fire lent an element of danger to our sport. Fear of stray shots kept us from climbing right to the top of the huge piles. But, having climbed as far as we dared, we would turn to leap down toward the beach in giant strides. The steps my sister took were fifteen feet from jump-off to landing. I spent most of that time just sliding down the slope on my backside. My sister was close to flying. She leapt further, bruised herself, got hung up in tree branches . . .

I stroked harder. The gravel pyramids had changed shape drastically since I was a child. The land was now fenced.

Children could no longer push the limits of safety here. It has to be about jumping off, I decided. At last I had my chance. This would be my own attempt to challenge the conveyer belt of life . . .

At last I let a thrust of the paddle blades push away memory until it faded behind me into the misty November atmosphere. I slowed to a stop. The water began to hiss with rain. I drifted, a leaf afloat in a great vastness of ocean. Subliminally I sensed strange currents luring me outward. I blinked as I looked into the rain. In front of me a loon had surfaced. Its haunting call echoed over the expanse of water. We shared the sound that seemed suddenly to metronome the rhythm of all life. I sat transfixed, my paddle resting on the deck. If only the moment could last, I thought, and reached into my lifejacket pocket to yank out my pencil and the sheets of paper I planned to use for a logbook.

As I fumbled the paper fell onto the wet deck. I tried to dry it off on my salty lifejacket; it only got wetter. I broke the point of my pencil as it jabbed a hole through the damp sheets.

There was no way to trap any of the moments here, I realized, as the kayak lurched and I made a swipe with the paddle just in time to stop a capsize. I still had a lot to learn. I went back to sitting still and the boat settled down. The loon dove, then rose again, teasing. Around me lay the world of water, beckoning me into the exquisite heart of a painting, but I didn't have the skills to touch it. The ocean was making me an offer; I had almost missed seeing it. It would take time to hone my skills for sketching in a bobbing, floating studio, but yes, there was no reason why I couldn't ride that conveyer belt of life now, I thought. Subject matter for painting was out there. I wouldn't need to stay with painting boats and harbours. Using the kayak as a method, I could paint the things that were closer to my heart.

Move out into the waterscape, whispered the rain. Sense my call if you will, cried the loon. I can take you to where painting would be meaningful — truthful, offered the kayak.

We drifted loonwards, kayak and I, and the loon dove

again and left me the silence of deep thought. When it surfaced again, I backed away until eye contact was broken. Beyond the loon a rainbow stretched end to end from the ocean across the spit of land to the lagoon behind me.

Omens, I thought, as I lifted my paddle and struck out again and the strange current caught the Nordkapp like a small crumb of flotsam and drew it onward into a new direction, toward the mainstream.

# 4.  Raven Christening

 NAMES HAD come easily to my other boats, *Loon* and *Soulcatcher*, but for some reason a name for my shiny yellow kayak was not so easily gained. And then a surprising spring adventure changed all that.

I had been given a tow rope by my kayaking teacher, and since I was building a sundeck at the time, I decided to put my kayak to work in a mission to beachcomb for two five-foot beams. That way I would be combining a pleasant outing with a work mission. I packed my sketchbook. I would miss nothing.

A large amount of lumber from old containment walls and docks flushes around the coastal shores, moved by rising and falling tides following winter storms. Eventually it finds its way even into protected waters like Saanich Inlet. I anticipated finding just what I wanted. On board I carried a crowbar, a hammer and a pruning saw.

I travelled along in good spirits, entertained by, but wary of a transient sea lion who seemed to be enjoying my company. He rolled in and out of the water beside me with all the grace of a true water lover. Ahead of me as I passed Tsartlip Point I noticed an Indian elder sitting on a log at the top of the beach. His eyes followed my kayak and its companion as they sliced the water keenly and gracefully.

Were the watercraft he had known in his youth making a parade of memories over his eyes? I wondered, as I drew in close to the bay. Early Indian canoes were hollowed out logs, narrower even than the boat I travelled in. I remembered when I was a child those canoes had landed on our beach on nights when tides were low enough to yield a harvest of clams. I would creep to the window beside my bed and watch as the lanterns and the campfires lit the beach, throwing images of the diggers against the burnished wood of the canoe hulls. Morning would find the sand upheaved. A few charred sticks and distinct grooves would be all to show that the clam gatherers had come and gone.

I passed close in to shore. My boat, I knew, was not designed from a hollow log. Its forebears had come from a far off land where logs were unknown. They had been made of skins sewn over a frame of sticks. All in all, I thought, the sea lion had the best of all designs.

The Indian elder did not smile as I passed; he just looked solemn. I drifted by without waving, knowing the gesture would be meaningless to the old man. We shared only the moment in each other's awareness before passing. His eyes were on tiny Senanus Island ahead of me. Once an Indian mortuary place, the island now stood bathed in soft light by mists that had blued the hills for weeks.

My thoughts returned to my boat. Skins and sticks or not, it should have a name, one that befit the traditions of the Inuit boat from which her design had come, and something to depict her role as catalyst for yet unborn paintings of the west coast of British Columbia. Nothing yet had come to mind.

I moved out into a cross wind and let the wave action, quartering, tease the bow of my new craft. The sea lion faded away into the depths while a fast modern launch passed in front of me and I crossed its wake.

I rounded the island and pulled ashore on a sheltered beach, put the boat above the tide and fetched out my tea before setting out to look for the beams I wanted. Feeling the edge of hunger from the exercise of paddling, and a certain idleness settle like a spell upon me, I let teatime blend into lunchtime. I removed my sandwich from my pack, but kept a decadent cinnamon bun stowed behind the seat in the cockpit. The bun would be my reward when the woodhunting job was complete.

While I sat in the silent morning munching on my cheese sandwich, I began to hear strange noises emanating from the interior of the island. I stopped chewing to listen. There were clicking sounds behind me up on the bank. I looked all around and tried to rationalize them — it wasn't that large an island — but what? *Indian mortuary place* came back to mind, a picture of bodies placed in trees. I had read they did that on many of the small coastal islands of British Columbia near old villages. I had read somewhere that the bones years later would tumble out onto the ground below . . .

I began looking for movement in the scrub that lined the rocky banks, but saw nothing. I sat, not eating, and I heard it again. The sounds were louder, more distinct this time. An image of bones rattling as they hung down from trees bothered my mind.

I thought of the elder I had seen, with his eyes pinned on the tiny island framed by rising mist. What had he been

looking at? Strange things could happen at any time on a
mortuary island, my mind prodded — but no . . .

The arbutus has a way of struggling through the
evergreens. Its trunks get twisted into contorted shapes as the
evergreens grow faster, stealing light. There was a grove of
arbutus on Senanus Island. Their distorted shapes tortured the
landscape of the little island. I looked up the bank through
the twisted tangle and sat clutching the half-eaten sandwich. I
no longer had a taste for it.

My eyes caught the shadow over the sun with a sudden
shiver — and was that the moon up in broad daylight? Did the
strange sounds have something to do with the sighs of the
souls of long-dead Indians? Of course not, I rationalized, as I
shifted positions, hair prickling the back of my neck. Enough,
I decided, leaping up to cross the tiny beach, then back
again, while the sun pierced the fog that drifted past.

I came back to my kayak. Without yet a scratch on her
fresh wax, she gleamed cheerfully in the light. In the six
months I had owned her, I had learned to look on her as
company and friend. Why let my imagination play games with me?

Up in the trees a shadow darted. When I looked I could see nothing, nothing out of place. "Voodoo and magic," I said bravely. "And I'd better get on with finding the driftwood I want." I set out up the rocks.

On top of the tideline, almost as if by magic, the wood was there; I found a sound two-by-four amongst the drift, then a battered four-by-four. Thanks to heavy winter storms wood was abundant this year. Pieces of docks and rafts were everywhere.

The job of dragging the wood to the kayak bolstered my courage. The noise would frighten away anything, even Indian spirits. When I got to the boat and looked the wood over carefully, I realized that although the beams were the right thickness, they were not long enough to suit the needs for the job I had in mind. I decided not to take them, but to hide them in the deep bush at the top of the rocks for retrieval another day.

The sunlight now flooded the island through the last traces of mist. Ribbons of its shadows danced across the twisting arms of the arbutus trees around me. Working had relaxed the grip on my nerves — but only for a moment. Something dropped with an audible plop and a flicker of shadow near my feet. I leapt a mile. This was the last straw! Without looking I took flight, plunged out of the bush over the rocks, knowing my kayak would be gone or smashed. I would be at the mercy of the spirit world . . . Slipping and scrambling, I landed in a heap below the rocks not twenty feet from my boat. From ground level I looked up, knowing that some horrible spectre . . .

There, sitting on my kayak coaming happily molesting the last few crumbs of what had once been my cinnamon bun, squatted a large black raven.

I sat up on the heap of stones and clay that had come down the bank with me. The raven was laughing, I was sure of it.

With a graceful hop he leapt up a few feet into the air, dropped some crumbs and gracefully came back down onto the kayak. His eyes shone like black beads and focused on the silver Raven bracelet on my wrist. He seemed to look me over rather carefully. His large shiny beak clicked. I remembered the large beaked Haida Raven drawings that my friend Doug had sketched for me on a long ago visit to Skidegate in the Queen Charlotte Islands. A flood of memories came back, the Skidegate Beach ravens . . . And Dick, the bracelet artist who had told me of the legend, how Raven had stolen the moon from the chief's magic box and had thrown it into the sky, where it stays to this day.

The Trickster hopped up onto the nearest twisted branch of arbutus. He upstaged the broad daylight moon behind him in the sky. In one glance I took in the boat, the raven and the moon! *"Raven Moon,"* I thought. "I'll call my kayak *Raven Moon."*

# 5.  One Hundred and Ten

 I CAME to journey further and further from my home port of Deep Cove. Through paddling friends I discovered a wealth of material for painting. There were worlds I had never known out beyond the fringes of home waters. Turret Island is a place of enchantment, with a wooded forest and a rocky shoreline typical of the exposed coastline of British Columbia. Two miles long by half a mile wide, Turret Island lies in Barkley Sound, halfway up Vancouver Island's west coast in the archipelago known as the Broken Group Islands.

I first ventured into the waters of Barkley Sound with my teacher, who promised a wonderland of islands with sea caves and turrets and a wealth of places to explore out of season and away from the crowd. I paddled *Loon*, my first kayak, and it was there that I was all but capsized by the lack of a seat against which I could brace myself. The perseverance and encouragement of my teacher and a certain memory of the woman tending the stove in a faded photograph helped me survive that first confrontation with the sea's fierceness. When at last I was truly capsized, I poked myself back into the boat and resolved to learn the eskimo roll.

After acquiring *Raven Moon* with her greater capabilities, I jumped at the chance to return with new

friends to the area. It soon became a yearly indulgence to travel there. Eventually I made my mind up to attempt a solo excursion. That way I would not distract friends by wanting to spend most of the time sketching and painting.

Only in Barkley Sound does my boat sing like this, I realized, as I listened to the faint notes of the bow and stern toggles swinging with movement along the curve of the swells as I dipped my paddle blades southward in the direction of Turret Island. I had left behind a lot of fetters that would have kept me at home in Deep Cove. Even though my children were grown and gone, there were lawns that needed mowing, gardens that demanded weeding and watering, to say nothing of my animals: ducks, dogs and cats. I shoved thoughts of responsibilities away with each deliberate stroke of my paddle. All sounds of humanity faded behind me as the cares of civilization thinned and fragmented, drifting away with the wake of my boat. The connections with mankind were severed. With that first thrust of the paddle sending me seaward I slid into the world of nature and wilderness. I had come a long way from the seatless boat that used to pearl dive into the waves. I had exactly what I wanted in *Raven Moon*.

The treasures I carried in *Raven Moon*'s hold were all I owned in the world at this moment: food, bedding, sketching things. I had walked out of my home without glancing back, lured by the sea, the islands and the kayak. It had been done before, I told myself; look at Ulysses — and he was gone seven years! How long I might be gone only the Fates could tell. When Ulysses returned to his home, the only one who

remembered him was his dog, I thought with a smile, and I had two dogs.

I swung out between the two Stopper Islands and into the open water, crossing directly to my destination. Although all islands are unique, worlds in microcosm, Turret Island intrigued me with the fragility of her existence. The early morning sea was calm with a long undulating swell. I could see Turret Island backlit in the distance, luring me to warmth and light and a wealth of sketching material. In *Raven Moon*'s watertight hatches I carried only the very basic requirements for survival: my bedding in the driest place on board, the forward hatch; the puptent I had bought from a friend for ten dollars; some clothing; my art supplies; my old Argus camera; and enough food to last for two weeks.

*Raven Moon* cut an arrow's path to my island destination on water that was as smooth as glass. Memory of once travelling a few inches of coast on logs in my teens teased my mind as I ventured forth on deep green water. I had come a long way from hiding in the bottom of a rowboat. There is a place one gets hooked, I thought, remembering the first day when my grandfather had taken me fishing, and then the days of paddling on logs and dreaming of going to sea. Next thing you know you are in a kayak and Nature comes calling the artist within you.

A distant group of gulls following the flotsam drift on the tide interrupted my thoughts. The birds were stretched out in a line in front of me as far as I could see, a barrier between me and Turret Island. I paddled as close as I dared, shipped my paddle and drifted toward them, my kayak sliding on the mirror of early morning.

I drifted, watching silently, waiting while drips from the paddle tinkled as they hit the water, made rings, then disappeared. Suddenly I crossed the range of tolerance. The chariest of the birds took flight and the rest followed. Cries rent the air, wings flapped, bullets of guano rained about me as the birds fractured the sky with their clamour and raucous cries. Fortunately the birds were bad shots. I watched the white daubs, like oil paint, disperse in a liquid silver bath just beyond *Raven Moon*.

Everything in nature was kind, I thought, as I dipped my paddle blades once more. The gulls resettled, a group of white specks on the drift far away. I wished I could have caught the scene, but it had happened so fast. It would not be easy to capture nature that moved so quickly on its own whims, I thought. Here was I, unprepared; my sketchbook was in the hold. Another problem I must somehow solve.

Somewhere between the birds and my destination the wind began to make itself known. First a vague shiver of gooseflesh prickled the surface of the water. Soon small chuckling waves shattered the early morning mirror and a good breeze was drying my lips, flapping my hat brim and tugging at the bow of *Raven Moon*. Before long there were two-foot peaks atop the low swells. I forgot about art and began the hard work of leaning into the wind and closing upon my destination with a determined hand.

Passing through one of the narrow channels that sever Sisters Four, Turret, Trickett and the two Lovett Islands, I slipped out onto the open coast, where the swells come bounding in over four thousand miles of open water from Japan. I looked west and wondered where the line was that divided east from west. All I had been taught in school atlases seemed to fade away into insignificance. Japan was there, exotic and far away; I simply couldn't see it. And it was certainly off the map of an artist's budget, I told myself. I might never see it. Had I stayed working in the bank where I was at twenty, I might have made the trip soon enough, but leaving secure income was a trade-off when time became the precious commodity. If I wanted to paint, it looked like I would have to sacrifice my visions of seeing the far-off world. But that's alright, I told myself, I'll just look deeply into the world that surrounds me, the immediate one.

As I schussed down toward the beach where I would make camp, barely submerged rocks bared their teeth on either side. My constant vigil was required for the little telltale swirls of white water that might leave me stranded on pinnacles of rock in the troughs of waves. The immediate world was demanding enough, I thought, as I turned the corner of the Turret Island promontory and washed out free of the swells. Under my paddle power I coasted up the silent inlet and nudged the shore.

I clambered out onto the grassy midden, scavenged for short pieces of wood to use as rollers so that I could pull my boat ashore without scraping it over rocks and barnacles, then after turning around three times like a dog flattening the tall grass of his genetic past, I set about raising camp. With the sun out I soon converted nearby bushes to a good laundry rack and hung all the pieces of my wet kayak gear. A colourful display of pink woollies and ragged camp clothes can be far more interesting on a bush than at the laundromat downtown, I decided, as I stood back to draw the scene.

By late afternoon I was feeling smug with the success of my adventure and took my sketching things along the shore to look for subject matter. The spot I chose was full of driftwood. It had collected for so many years that the underlayer had rotted down to a dry, dark garden. New hemlocks had sprouted and gained a foothold among the logs. The hidden underlayer had become the home of mice and martens and small grey birds. One can be lulled in this garden into thinking of perpetual summer, I thought, as I settled down on a log that was mostly chaff and got out my pen and paper to draw the scene.

In front of me as I sat, grasses moved gently in soft

summer air. Beyond their fringe small islets seemed to float in
the vista of sea offshore. I watched them turning in the
evening light from green to brown, and the sky to gold. I
drew the outlines and shaded them with my pen. But once
again Nature charged things with rapid movement. Nature
was a constant pulse, while the lines I had drawn were static,
lifeless somehow, and dead. What I drew did not seem to
express that movement of colour and light that was the wind
in the grasses of Turret Island.

I worried the sketch a few more times, and the more I
worried the lines the more I turned to dreaming and
dissatisfaction. I had come a long way for this. I had expected
my drawings to be rich and full, and here I was wondering
what on earth I could draw that would express the nature
around me. I found my dream broken by small birds that
came to pick in and out through the logs. They were
followed by a marten, who paused directly in front of me. I
saw his whiskers twitch at the presence of the large stranger.
They moved. Whenever I looked they moved again, and I
could capture none of it; I only got the whiskers drawn
before the marten was gone.

I sat motionless, my pen poised in a trap of hesitation. I was a beginner in art — only a beginner, I told myself. I had miles to go and only half a life left. How was I going to do it when I couldn't even get started?

The marten moved on. There was nothing so still and quiet as the black lines I had drawn. What was missing? I looked out again on the darkening islands and through a peach sky to the far horizon. Japan beckoned. Suddenly I latched onto a memory of bringing home a library book as a young girl. It was called *Hokusai Manga* and had pages that were double, folded rice paper, and on every page were the drawings of people and animals, all full of movement. The first drawings I had ever done were after looking into *Hokusai Manga*.

Hokusai, the artist, so thoroughly immersed himself into his art that he once remarked, "When I am ninety I shall have learned about the structure of nature. At one hundred I shall have penetrated the mystery of life. When I am one hundred and ten, everything I do, whether it be dot or line, will come alive."

I turned back to my drawings. I was a child in art, and it would take more than one lifetime for it all to come alive. I must get to work.

# 6.　Turret Island

TURRET ISLAND became a favourite of mine, in part at least, because each visit seemed to teach me something new, to provide some sort of revelation. Not all were as pleasant as my lesson on Hokusai; some were darker. The day I explored the hidden interior of the island was one of these.

Beside my camp a stream disappeared into the depths of a hemlock grove. I set out to explore it and found a series of still black pools that hid amongst the moss reflecting sky and the dark tops of trees. There was an eeriness about the place. Pooling in a black bog of disintegrated forest, devil's bathtubs, tiny sip wells that trickled and trembled with movement, so quiet the forest seemed deserted of all life.

As I stooped over one such pond seeking the sight of even the smallest of insects, I found the blackness disconcerting. There was nothing — nothing alive. Then suddenly my consciousness was drawn to a wriggling movement. I stared hard into the darkness of the water, saw it again. The trembling was coming from a large fist-sized globe of spawn. I leaned toward it, examining, sketchbook in hand. Numerous small tadpoles squirmed inside a wombed world of forest gelatin. I watched, transfixed. Frog spawn! Appearing to be protected, the tiny beings were in a most

precarious environment. Would they live long enough to burst forth, I wondered, or would they be eaten by other creatures? The summer was fast drying the pools, would leave the tadpoles stranded, turn them to hardpan, perhaps, before their first wild dash to freedom.

A sudden shiver of insight trembled at the edge of my thoughts. Nature doesn't care who gets caught. I pictured myself trapped somehow on a tiny island in the middle of a vast place. My attitude toward the day was changing. I left the strange ball, a hundred black wrigglers, moving, moving — but trapped. These embryos already marked frog would need to grow arms and legs in a hurry to defend themselves or to flee, if they were ever to make it to adulthood. They might as well have been flies in amber. Doom overshadowed and mocked their faint tremblings and exertions.

I would attempt to draw them, I decided; that might give them some posterity — if the drawing was good enough . . .

Being busy sketching would help to disperse the strange gloom that seemed suddenly to be rising like mist out of the silent wood to surround me.

I sat on the wet moss and began forming the globe of tiny life on paper. Beside me in the water was another globe; the moon had made its way through the dark high branches above me to frame a disk of a different sort in that same water that held the unmade frogs. An hour went by. The moon slipped behind a straggle of foliage overhead. I won't miss the moon, I thought, now that I have trapped her into my sketchbook. Time can move on. Nature has let me trap the slow-moving. If one had to keep warm by this noonday moon, one would feel her far too distant a thing; and yet she controlled such as the arrival of the orb of forest gelatin with the baby frogs.

I was cold when I got up; although my rainpants kept the water out, I realized they had become clammy and miserable. To prod circulation into stiff limbs I started moving up the creek, came to where it bubbled out from under the rocks of a subterranean crack. If I crossed the island I would come out onto the north shore and could make my way back by the beach to my camp.

I set out. I was soon breathless from hard struggling through heavy bush and over wet rocks. In this forest there was no path to follow, not even deer trails, only jungles of vines, fallen logs and straggly bush. I had pushed my way a few feet at a time and hoped I would not have to backtrack through the tangle I had left behind. At last I came out on a clearing where the sun shone down boldly into an open meadow. I was glad to shed the darkness of the woods. It wasn't long before I realized the open space was not a meadow at all, but a blowdown — an area where the wind had knocked out a whole grove of trees in one mighty breath. Winter storms are real on the west coast, I said to myself, not just what I have read about — not just what I have dreamed . . .

I imagined myself riding out the fury of a winter gale on the island. I watched sea drench land in a spume of white, was deafened by the thunder of the waves' engulfment. I pictured storms breaking their way overland to rejoin the sea

on the other side, taking a shortcut through trees and bush, breaking branches and trunks of tall stout hemlocks. I saw trees crash to earth, mowed down by the wind. Nature was a giant treading upon blades of grass . . .

The vision passed in a moment. I continued my struggle through the grove. I chose the stoutest trunk, grabbed a branch and hoisted myself up. As I did so the needles that had once been living hemlock tree came off in my hand. Life had been plucked from these trees in just a few moments of violence, I thought. Now roots poked skywards, out of their element. Death had dried them into skeletons and their flesh came off in my hands . . . I did not like this place. *Roots without earth, empty barren ground*; the words formed in my head. I tried to shove them away. In the interior of the island and myself, peace was gone. Hidden here was death and a great undoing. Turret Island was an idyllic place only on the outside and the visible edges told a lie of peace and harmony. What was real was inside.

I began struggling around projecting limbs, scrambling toward the small branches of their crowns, crossing to newer, cleaner trunks, and battling the jagged branches. I was

sweating inside the bindings of my rain clothes and all the while the needles, still green, fell over me like sand in an hourglass, touched down like feathers into my open palm to lie, tiny corpses, without breath, without life.

I shook them off as if I'd been stung. Storm and pestilence would come after me, too. What was I doing clinging to the top of a dying tree in an empty place with death stalking all the while? I began to crash carelessly over the dead limbs, falling off trunks into hollows, reaching, flailing; I cut my arms on sharp broken hemlock spikes. I hurried to escape the decay to get to the peace of the outside perimeter.

The beach on the north side was below a high bank that stopped me in my tracks. I would not retrace my steps through the blowdown! Somehow I must find a way to the beach. I noticed a tree trunk that leaned over the bank at a sharp angle to rest its top on the sandy shore. There was just enough of a slant for me to attempt to scramble down. I clambered onto it, fighting the tangle of my wet rainpants, scraping my arm, getting a whip in the eye for my efforts, and straining rib muscles. I inched along with no hands free to wipe at tears pricking pain in my eyes. My scraped skin burned furiously. Half blind, I struggled past upright branches one by one, seeking below each with a foot where I couldn't see for a secure stepping place, unsure at each step if the limbs would support my weight. If I fell to the beach in a heap of broken bones, who would care? Nature, least of all. If I injured myself, who would paddle for me? In those desperate moments I had lost all liking for Turret Island.

I stepped down where there was no foothold. Wildly I reached for the only thing to save myself from falling, a small green branch within reach of my straining fingers. I realized immediately the resilience of living wood. The length of wet trunk from here to the beach was covered in upright new trees!

I sat down where the broken crown touched the beach. Bathed in cool air, I sat staring at the young new growth. The tree that had fallen was a nursemaid; in dying it had become the catalyst for new life. Out of its top surfaces grew new hemlocks and moss was thick and green, centipedes crawled. The tree was both dead and alive.

I pulled out my sketchbook. Immediately I began to draw the nursemaid log; it's title already had formed in my mind. I'd call it *Life Cycle*.

At last, Nature was giving me a drawing that would count!

I walked the shore of Turret Island, pausing to look for the mice and the martens and the small grey birds that kept their dwellings hidden among the logs and trees. Turret Island is for the living after all, I told myself, not just for the dead.

# 7.   Holograms

TURRET ISLAND, with its neighbours Trickett and the two Lovett Islands, forms a chain of four. Native people say that Raven dropped clamshells as he flew and they became islands. Four of them had been strung out in a row in front of me like skipped stones. I picked the middle one, Trickett Island. My mind, in neutral, drifted back to a previous trip to Trickett Island, the day my friends and I had discovered the cave.

We had set out on foot under a barrage of rain. Philip, Mike and I had left our kayaks behind at the campsite on Turret Island in the hope of clearing weather and the chance of paddling later in the day. It was too wet even to think of sketching that day. We set out to enjoy exploring in fine detail the circumference of the island and to harvest some berries for supper.

In good spirits and whatever rain gear we could muster from our duffel bags, we crossed the drifted beach logs from our camp on Turret Island and waded the channel while the tide was low. Starting out on the south side, a place of shell beaches interspersed with rocky log-strewn outcroppings, we foraged among the dense walls of salal that overhung the shore in leathery green cascades. The purple blackberries burst in our mouths with just the right moment of ripeness. We felt rich in Nature's abundance; we did not feel the rain.

After lingering long enough to eat our fill from this wild food bank, we moved to the tip of a small spit that ran out to the west end of the island. The glare of the white shell was hard on the eyes, a *tromp l'oeil* of sun. We picked up driftwood poles and made a game of prodding at the shell and the drift for exoskeletons, undamaged snail shells, and then Japanese flotsam because it was plentiful. Lightbulbs embellished with characters we could not read, pieces of multi-coloured rope, and oblong plastic floats that appeared to have been scattered purely for our enjoyment.

"Those who are squeamish should not prod the beach rubble," said Philip sternly, interrupting the silence of our thoughts. "Did you know Sappho said that? Isn't it odd that a poem so old is just as current and meaningful today?"

We proceeded down the darker, north side of the island. The wind-driven rain, which had been at my back, now began to blur my glasses and dribble down my nose. I left my trophies behind in a row on a sodden log. I pulled my toque over my ears, bit down on the facing rain and walked behind my friends. Soon we encountered a wound in Trickett Island's side, which stopped us in our tracks. The sea had ground away the edges of the rocky shore into a chasm. The water swilled in and gurgled out. Nearby was a cave.

The cave did not compare with the high vaulted sea caverns of the outer islands in Barkley Sound, having neither the height nor the depth and majesty. Nor did it have the endless surge of the open coast or the pastures of bull kelp and the startled cormorants that flew into your face as you paddled in to peer into dark, mysterious recesses. How far could such cracks go into an island, I wondered? The big coast caves were cauldrons through which the dark waters swilled endlessly, and there was a danger that a kayaker could be heaved up on the height of the swells, only to be crushed against the ceiling and drowned.

I had now paddled many times in Barkley Sound with Philip and Mike, sometimes with others, sometimes just the three of us. I remembered once having persuaded Philip to

back his boat, *Fraifaxie*, into a small cleft in the rock. It was narrow enough that the walls could be clutched on either side to steady a kayak. I had wanted to photograph him. It was a dangerous place to be, but I asked him to hold the pose while I manoeuvred *Raven Moon* into position for a shot. Through the camera I saw a sudden look of horror cross Philip's face just as I jammed the shutter home. A swell had lifted him, boat and all clear of his handholds. It pushed him up the walls of the cave five feet until his head was within inches of the ceiling.

"It's a smashing shot!" I cried.

Philip's face had turned white . . .

"This looks about as far as we can go around Trickett Island," Philip said, breaking into my reverie. We stood looking at the twelve-foot surge of moving water between us and the opposite bank. The gap was too wide to leap.

"Nonsense," Mike said with a laugh. He began to clamber around the edge of the slick rock, pushing through heavy bush with one hand and clinging to the vertical stone surface with the other. Suddenly, with a loud splash, he was in the chasm up to his thighs. Laughing at his misfortune, he struggled out on the far side. "Come on," he called.

"We're only half his height, you and I," said Philip. "We'd never make it."

"Besides, there's a cave," I said as I looked back along the beach.

"Let's look at it then," agreed Philip. He knew that any cave should not be scorned or passed casually.

Mike waited for us. He would not come back.

The cave was low-ceilinged, barely visible under the bank. Stooping, we entered, pushing the overhanging vines out of our faces; they closed in after us, cutting us off from the sea and the rain and the rocky shore outside. We needed no flashlight, since the foyer was no longer than twenty feet. A dull gloomy light settled with the drooping of the vines like a breath of mist behind us. Stooping over, we pushed our way to the farthest reaches, turned, and looked back the way we had come. All around me I could hear the soft dripping of the eaves from the depths of the tiny vault. Dimly I could make out the movement of water falling onto small shiny pebbles of quartz and black stones. Obviously high tides could find their way right to the back walls, I realized, could sweep out the flotsam and polish the stones to pure gems.

The moment transported me into a prehistoric world. Crouched in her depths, squatting like a wedge between floor and wet ceiling, all the caves in which my ancestors had lived drew around me to engulf me and pull me back through the centuries.

Gradually I began to hear something in the rock akin to a muffled pounding. Was it the surf booming far off on the coast rocks outside? Or was it something even deeper than that, I wondered? Could it be the heartbeat of the island itself, beating out its primordial rhythm? I looked around at Philip to see if he was hearing it, too, but the rapt attention on his face stopped me from voicing the question. He must have been hearing the muse speaking through Sappho. We stayed only a moment; it could have been an eon.

"What did you find?" called Mike from across the chasm.

All I could say was connected to sketching and painting, but how, in the rain? What could I say? "A big leaky umbrella."

With a laugh Mike made a sweeping gesture toward the water-filled channel. "Are you coming?" He stood leaning on a large stick, his blue anorak welded to his body. He had given up caring about the wet. He was waiting now to enjoy our attempt at crossing.

"The water would be up to our necks," said Philip. Then, turning to me, he said, "Why don't we try crossing the island instead of retracing our steps? I've always wanted to see what the interior of Trickett Island is like."

"Mike, we'll cut across and meet you at the channel in about twenty minutes," I called across the chasm.

"We could scramble up right here," said Philip, grabbing a root and looking up the bank into a jungle of growth.

I heard Mike's laugh, and a muffled "Goodbye." I wondered if he hadn't muttered, "Fools," just as a large wave had shot up the chasm and swallowed the stones. I didn't wait to find out, but followed Philip. He was already climbing hand over hand, making bannisters of some twisted roots that wound out of the soft crumbly earth under the trees.

"This isn't easy," I muttered, as I spat out the chaff that was pouring down on me from Philip's feet and from the fragile net of needles and soil that he was disturbing. "The bush sticks like wires and hooks," I said, as I untangled a snagging whip of growth and wet leaves from my collar.

"Like Afro hair," said Philip. "But surely no one has set foot here before us. How many places are there left on earth where man hasn't yet set foot? Perhaps we're the very first."

Eyes full of dark earth crumbs and wet hair showering black dandruff-like effluvia, we gained a small headway, perhaps a deer trail, and stooping, pushed branches out of our faces, regained the beach and set out to meet Mike at the appointed place.

"That's strange," I said, after a moment, as I looked out toward the coast on what I thought was the south-facing shore. "The offshore islands look almost the same as they do on the north side, don't they? I hadn't noticed that before."

"Yes, they do, don't they? But nature's full of repetition,"

said Philip. "One place can look remarkably like another; I've always thought so when I'm sailing. Look! Someone's been here already today!"

Philip was pointing to fresh tracks on the wet shore. "I didn't think there would be anyone else around; the weather has been so unsuitable for camping this year."

"It isn't just Mike, is it?" We followed the tracks until after a moment, like the Raven's clamshell, the penny dropped. "We've crossed a promontory, that's all — not the island! We're only thirty yards from where we went in!"

We were fools; Mike had been right! "Mike will think we're lost," said Philip. "We'd better hurry, or he'll think we've deserted him."

"He'll give up in disgust."

We found Mike standing at the waterline staring at the tide as it rose steadily in the channel. His toque poured little rivulets down his chin. His beard bristled with a rime of waterdrops. Philip and I tried to explain, but Mike merely laughed at us. "Fools" must still have been there under his breath.

We stood for a moment examining the sorry state. We could only laugh at ourselves as we hesitated before the channel, now at full flood.

"Well, why worry about our boots?" Mike grinned. "We'd never get them back on over our wet socks anyway." He stepped into the water.

"Right," we agreed. In a phalanx we forded the channel, fully dressed. Then we squelched back to our most welcome camp, where there was a fire to be lit and hot cocoa and Peppermint Schnapps.

Today was a different day. The sun was out and everything was brilliant in the morning light. Negative spaces among the trees were rich and dark and full of birds. *Raven*

*Moon* danced across the waves and pulled me down the north side of Trickett Island once again.

As I approached the sea chasm I paddled in toward shore. If I was in luck, with the waves in this direction, I would find a place on the nearby beach with enough protection for easy landing; my heart stepped up its beat. I would explore the cave again. Swinging in close to the rocks I caught the rising swell, then my heart stopped altogether; I peered in disbelief up the beach. The overhang was there, and the dark shape, the vines, but the cave was nowhere to be seen!

Paddling back and forth, trying to force my mind to grasp this new emptiness, all I could see were boulders the size of footstools, which no human hand could have moved!

The ocean pushed me upward on the swells, downward into the troughs. I stared from above, then from below. Why couldn't the swells stop for a minute and just let me sit in one place and try to assimilate what had happened?

It was as if the cave had never existed. I could only rationalize that winter storms had filled it in. Into my mind unbidden came the memory of the friends with whom I had shared a day in the rain. They were gone, too. Today, at least, I was alone. At last I turned away, swallowing sadness, aware that I no longer shared the heartbeat I once had known with this tiny island, my friends, and the small cave.

I headed back to camp. As I moved around to face the incoming swells, voices from that past returned. Those memories, now purified by the wind, no longer contained the misery of that rainy day, only the joy of companionship. Oddly enough, on later trips I would seek and find the cave again, but on this day as I rode back to camp I caught a glimpse of my friends. They danced across my sight in lasting holograms of pleasure.

## 8.   Sea Lions and the Sail Rock Dream

I HAD been gaining in confidence with each trip. I was beginning to know the moods of *Raven Moon* and the wild flights of her fancy. When my mind wasn't on the sea, it was out in space where the eagles flew, weaving above the twisted grey skeletons of coast trees that wind and time distorted. This to me was the soul of what should be painted and I was learning to truly enjoy the escape from the day-to-day existence of working in a studio. I had grown increasingly hungry for the scenery of the west coast. Like a child in a candy store, the more I saw, the more I wanted to see.

I went to the wildest places I could find, the outer coast where I could hear the boom of surf and watch the wild birds embroidering trails over the islands as they rode the thermals. Earth-born and water-borne, my head was in the clouds in a place where I felt real freedom, where meaning seemed to come into my life and where I had a choice of islands to explore. This was Barkley Sound.

*Raven Moon* was certainly the choice way for me to travel in my journey of life, I thought, as I pushed off from Turret Island. Today I would make for the outer coast. Responding on cue, my kayak slipped away from shore with a gentle hiss of

sand. I flexed the arms of my life with the paddle and began on my journey, the first of ten thousand strokes.

Hopeful that calm weather would prevail, I paddled into a still grey dawn; a gentle low swell was on the water. With this morning coolness I predicted there would not be the brisk westerlies that often accompanied warm afternoons in summer. In my pockets was paper for sketching. If subject matter presented itself where I couldn't go ashore, I would attempt again to sketch right in the boat. For extra insurance I also carried an instamatic camera; if I could not put down the paddle, I would still have a chance to capture a subject.

Off the port bow from Turret Island as you face the chain of four lie sister islands, Clarke and Benson, parallel, and similar in size. Between them the swells sometimes roll in high over a shallow entrance. Going through in the middle can be a roller coaster ride. The early morning mist had turned into isolated patches. Kelp was turning the place gold.

Benson Island is a forty-three-acre remnant of pioneering days. It once had a hotel and ten acres of cleared land with a cultivated orchard and garden. Now it is a wild jungle obscured by forest. Half-hidden by deep bush is an old cement reservoir. The water is still fresh and clean, as if the island expected the return of its people. As I stooped with my waterbottle at the clear jewel-like supply, my thoughts turned to the vulnerability of people who travel in kayaks. Time and distance can be foes of inestimable proportions. One must have good arms and a head to guide them, especially travelling solo.

I fanned mosquitoes away with my free hand as I propped the bottle between my feet, tightened the lid, and dusted off my gathering collection of memories of Barkley Sound. Then I looked at the tangled forest around me. A clump of golden mushrooms billowed out from a rotten log close to my feet. Oyster mushrooms, I thought, as I put down my canteen and took out my knife. Those are supposed to be delicious! But I stopped. If they were wrongly identified they might put an end to me at once. I mustn't be lured by their golden colour, their culinary look and my penchant for yellow foods: squash, custard, duckeggs, sweet potato. I pocketed my knife and took out paper and pen. Figuratively, where was I to draw the line? Was I too going to flirt with fate? Better be an artist, not a connoisseur of fine food . . .

While I sketched the rich golden horde, below me and out of my conscious sight the tide receded. When I strode out of the woods into the sunlight I found *Raven Moon* high above an acre of barnacle-covered boulders, the water still receding. I began searching for driftwood; I would have to drag the kayak over the top or scratch her to pieces on the rocks. Hadn't I learned anything about tides?

The sun made the flag of Japan as the calmness of the weather led me to choose going out the entrance and rounding Benson Island to the outside coast. As I turned outward, ahead of me lay Sail Rock, a small pinnacle that sat by itself.

Sail Rock was a familiar landmark. Striking in its solitariness, it squatted on what appeared to be a sea of infinity, like an ageless Buddha. White trailers of waves that had crossed from the Orient were turned aside by its sudden bulk. Over its head a coronet of birds circled timelessly. I was

drawn to make two strokes toward her, but then I veered off.
Staring at the Buddha was going to be enough. I remembered
the story of Daruma, who meditated so long that spiders,
making cobwebs, knitted his eyelids closed. The thought
turned me into an insignificant dot on a vast sea. Should I
drown in an instant, I thought, Buddha would not bat an eye,
nor be mindful of me. I was too wrapped up in my own life,
and although I sought freedom I was still afraid. I
remembered a recent dream: I had been trapped on that same
rock, which had become the archetypal rock to me. Clinging
to the cold grey iron stone, the seas swirled up to suck at my
feet, only to plunge away with a laughing roar. The ocean of
the dream had been a moat around me. I had tried to paint the
scene later, in the harsh light of day, but nothing could portray
the cold sweat that had overcome me during that night.

Now I had the chance to shout at Daruma with the
cobweb eyes. "I have no intention of penetrating the gates to
your impervious fortress!" I heard my own voice, the squawk
of a seabird drowned by the coast roar. It was a joke. I must
be losing my mind, I thought, and felt a fool as if the
wilderness was listening to my faint chirpings against a place
so wide, so loud. . . I veered away and left Sail Rock thrashing
its surf far off over my right shoulder.

I paddled on like a waterstrider concentrating on only its tiny space of pond. The swells of the exposed water began to flush me along rapidly; they caught *Raven Moon* at the stern and raised her high like a deliberate push of fate. As the waves surged, I rode forward on a swing seat, out over the air only to sink back rapidly, losing momentum. I braced with each wave and forced the boat back in line until my arms felt as though they would be torn from their sockets.

There was worse to come on this day. As I passed Combe Rock I was confronted by rebounding waves along the panhandle of my destination, Waower Island. Tossed hither and yon on the confused seas, I now braced not only for swells, but to keep upright and away from kelp beds. I tried paddling a little farther out from the shark tooth-shaped waves. One still had to keep some thread of control. I felt *Raven Moon* in an intractable mood, fighting for her head to turn me broadside.

In a violent explosion of surf over a hidden rock my head fairly burst. "Peril on the Sea" surged forth unbidden. An old school hymn had risen to give me courage. It was all I could do to sing away the devils at the top of my lungs, but it helped me to repress fear, to ride the seas clear to the corner of Waower Island.

Then I saw Sea Lion Rocks, behind them a small patch of water out of the wind. I made a run for its protection. For a few moments I breathed free. It was sanctuary. Then I saw the statues on the rocks, they decked the rocky pinnacle — a herd of sea lions! They were all poised on the verge of crashing down into the sea beside me. I respected their territory and gave them as wide a berth as was possible in the small calm pond of the rock's protection. I promised them that they were entitled to their private lives if I could gain sanctuary for only a few moments before going on. But I made the mistake of looking back to make sure they were not following. It was then that *Raven Moon* speared a large bull. It had been sleeping amidst a weedy blanket of green. With eyes closed, he had not seen the approach of a jousting kayak.

The bull dove in a roar of his own surf. *Raven Moon* washed sideways in great fright. I was bathed now in the culmination of adrenalin from a whole morning of fear. I knew in an instant the bull could dump me into the water as easily as I might tip unwanted tea down the sink. I was reduced to a quivering jellyfish.

He rose again not fifteen feet away, close enough for me to count the bristling whiskers that twitched on his face. I could smell his halitosis. I couldn't move for trembling. We eyed one another as the moments flowed by in the worst of slow motion. Out of the corner of my eyes I saw behind him the herd of cows plunge into the water and rush over as if they were entering the grandstand of an arena.

In battle I knew I was a certain loser because, even wearing my kayak, I had neither their bulk nor their posturing ferocity; but I also knew that flight would turn me into prey. Unable to flee, I tried to stare him down, as he was doing to me. As I looked deeply into the bovine eye, I recognized how much we were one and the same. I saw fear and the slight movement of retreat. In a flash I knew the school bully was just as scared as I.

The fear dissipated as we carefully back-paddled and the distance grew between us. As if by magic, a path opened before me, and I, a wee stranger among giants, was able to pass through the blubbery herd, to leave, quietly, and by the back door.

In a moment of new-found power as I departed, I called back that I recognized that neither *Raven Moon* nor I came anywhere close to their own fetid magnificence. If they would not pursue I would forever owe the sea lions a debt. It is easy to joke when the stress is released at last. I headed into the wild water with great thankfulness and travelled toward my destination of Waower Island as fast as I could.

I did not get swept down the coast in the direction of the Baja, nor into the great cup of Cape Flattery. I braced at just the right moment on the rising wave and turned *Raven Moon* around the edge of the island to give the whole scene at the corner of Waower Island a wide and shuddering berth, all the crashing, swilling sea that was a salad of weeds and boulders with a chilled, watery dressing. There was no need for a crouton, I called out — no need . . .

# 9. Waower Island Mystery

I DRIFTED into a bay of calm and softly undulating water just deep enough to float a kayak, the antithesis of the outside coast. Ahead of me lay a white shell berm glistening like an oasis in the morning sun. I made for it and, stepping ashore, tied *Raven Moon*'s mooring rope to a log. I collapsed among the shells and took out my flask of Benson Island springwater and some date loaf. I had certainly earned a rest; my arms would be sore for days. Enjoying the soothing qualities of the drink and a brief respite, I noted the sun had broken through the cloud of morning to tinge everything with colour. Rocks had turned from grey to raw sienna. Trees had turned to Windsor green, then burnt umber, their trunks absorbing light like velvet. Sea birds had become two-toned. In this landscape *Raven Moon* shone brilliant yellow, picking up highlights from the weed. She dazzled my eyes as I concentrated on her, a tiny craft that had brought me this miracle of place and empowerment.

Lulled by my rest after the exertion in the wild water and the confrontation with fear, I began to think if I weren't such a restless one, I would lie on the Waower Island beach all day soaking up the warmth that was reflecting from the white shell underfoot. But then, thought I, if restlessness were not my nature, I would not be here at all. So I broke my reverie and pulled the folded paper from my pocket, and began a sketch. However, it didn't satisfy me; such a scene demanded colour. I went to my boat and pulled out the roll of watercolour paper that I had squeezed into the hatch. With my small box of paints I went to work, furiously capturing the wild sunlit colours of the landscape that were emphasized by the sun-yellow dye of the focal point, *Raven Moon*. It was one of those rare paintings that forms itself before I begin and rolls off the brush in a moment of pure poetry. Within an hour it was done.

I came out of my reverie and set about busily exploring the shell bank, an obvious Indian midden. The bay had once been cleaned of rocks to make way for Nootka canoes. Its shoulders were white with the clamshells of past habitation. Above the bank in a cleft between the rocks was a small, narrow valley, protected from the wind and broad enough for canoe parking and storage. The bank was held together by the tall green beach grass that is used to this day in Nootka basket making. It grew tall enough to hide canoes and even man himself from unwanted intruders.

I walked into the rock cleft, marvelling that in some ancient age Waower Island had split almost in two. For a moment my imagination saw the white strength of countless winter storms slashing the crippled wind-bent trees with a deafening roar as it widened the crack. By this time of year the Indian people would have gone inland to safer camps, to the protected side of Effingham Island, which used to be known as Village Island. Why stay here and be blown out of the crack like the last few autumn leaves? Within the cleft I found pools and stopped to look in them for signs of life. They were rich red-brown, heavy with salt that rimed the edges white in patterns of crystal. The devil surely bathed here in the summertime, I thought, as my feet clattered over the craggy stones, the landscape like the pitted surface of the moon. Then I came out suddenly onto the open coast, the far-off sound of the sea lion rookery making music on the wind. The rumblings of those living behemoths gave a staccato beat to the ongoing roar of the open Pacific. The swells smashed on the rocks below me and splashed my face with scattered droplets. Sheets of water cascaded, leaving the glint and flash of white water over underwater forests, and turned the rocks that held up Waower Island into palm-covered atolls. I stared at the foaming lather. How could seaweed grow in such a disturbing environment as this?

I made an attempt to draw the toothy grin of water with its waving submarine palm trees. I tried to make sense of the sea on paper as it rose to explode through the cleft behind me in imagined winter storms. What a surge that must be! But how could I paint this roar that was more sound than sight, where Nature sang and vibrated in total wildness? How would I portray it? There would be a lot of white paper to leave as I harvested this light!

I stayed an hour, maybe two, sitting in a make-believe moonscape, absorbed by a scene in which time ceased to exist. Suddenly a bee found its way down from its sunlit flight to settle on my knee. I watched it turn three hundred and sixty degrees and fly off again, a frail fragile dot in a wild galaxy, and my knee only a compass rose, and only for an instant.

The bee's flight brought me back to the present. I gathered my flotsam and walked back up to the warm ponds, past the contorted bare branches and trunks of the twisted trees, past the hard sharp wall of pale green iron, the impenetrable needled affront to the edge of land. *Let not so much as a hand come into it*, the rush of audible air seemed to say to me . . . Well, put that in your painting, I thought, and stopped to add three more jagged knuckles to the old white limbs I had drawn.

I pocketed my paper at last and began scouting along the edges of the bush for traces of Indian life. Long I had wished to be in contact with the inhabitants who had first peopled the coast. What stories they might tell. I searched as if I might one day stumble on them, as if I might one day shoot back through time, as I often did in my dreams, to the villages of the coastal fringe. As I returned along the rock crack, my eyes swept the midden. There could be a stone hammer . . . lying in the bank, or buried under tons of salt and crumbled rock, or it could be hidden in the sheltered bank of grass and shell, deep, deep — and yet the small stones of the beach on the sheltered side appeared to lie undisturbed; they were still here . . . I couldn't remember for how long I had searched, hoping that one day I would stumble on one of the tools of the first peoples.

In the clear area tucked in behind the rock crack, again I saw the path where the stones had been moved. Had canoes really been hidden here? From what were the people hiding?

I recalled what I had read of the raiding, warring past, the days of lookouts and surprise raids. On Waower Island there seemed to be no answers to my questions.

Well, no harm in looking for a stone hammer, said the collector in me as I prowled along the top of the bank poking through the grasses and white shell.

I came back to where *Raven Moon* sat blistering in the hot open pocket of the bay. The tide was now on the flood, and the pond with its barnacled pebbles was being filled in quickly. In an hour or so I'd be able to step into *Raven Moon* right where she was at the top of the beach and just paddle off. My arms didn't want to drag a boat; they still ached from bracing against the swells of the morning. If I just waited there would be no work to it. I would take half an hour and walk toward the east. I scrambled up over drift ten feet high. In the midst of the rubble I found the pontil of an old Japanese fishing float. It was lying in a nest of green glass fragments. It was so thick it hadn't shattered, four inches across by an inch and a half deep, and this was only the pontil! The ball itself must have been more than a foot across, and it must have floated intact from Japan before it arrived only to smash on this strange wild island so far from home.

I remembered a story then about a Greenland kayaker who left shore to hunt for his starving people. Trapped upon an ice floe he drifted for days and landed by chance on the shores of the Outer Hebrides. He died there, in a strange world, cut off forever from the environment he knew.

I picked up the pontil. I would take it home, encase it in lead came and hang it in a window. When the light filtered through it, I'd be reminded that the ocean brings cultures close, brings things on the tides that are sometimes unexplainable and mysterious.

Above the high drift was an impenetrable wall of salal. I could go no further. My eyes darted along its edges until they focused on a small hole at the base of the bush. I wanted to go on. Stooping, I pushed myself through the tangles into a low-slung bushy corridor which broke out suddenly into a small open grove.

I knew immediately that I was in the remains of someone's camp. There was a semi-circle of old stones that had recently shaped a fireplace. Tatters of canvas tied to a branch suggested the remnants of shelter. Over the stones of the fireplace hung a kettle, low down and close to the blackened coals. With my eyes adjusting to the dim light, I saw an iron frying pan of enormous dimensions. It was not the sort that would have come in the usual light duffel of the average kayaker or canoeist, I thought, as I heaved it up off the ground. It was a pan that would have dwarfed the rings of any electric range, but it would have done fine for the flapjacks of a cowboy roundup. A large collection of needles plucked from overhead trees by the trembling of ocean air against dense forest had been deposited inside it, ready to be grilled for the next meal.

I was standing in the heart of a mystery that wanted solving. I looked around for other traces of habitation: a matted wet sleeping bag knotted among wild roots, cutlery, a disintegrated bag of tins of Campbell's soup together with a large wooden ladle on the dark forest floor. The tins had all but lost their calligraphy to spreading rust. I picked up the cleanest looking can and read, "Mu-room." A glass bowl shaping a crescent moon lay half in and half out of the bank.

Who was the camper, I wondered. Where was he now? Why did he come here in the first place, bringing such heavy supplies? Was he hiding? Did the huge pan suggest a group rather than just a solitary camper? Someone had been planning to live on soup warmed in a giant pan and served in a large glass salad bowl. Was it all he or she had been able to

run off with? All that could be grabbed or stolen? There had been rumrunners on this coast in the days of prohibition. Could there be drug runners?

I began to find items of clothing that my first search had missed: a pair of rotting grey wool worksocks which the bugs had made into a condominium, an unrecognizable drab green thing of coverall material. I scrambled around looking for more clues, but the search was impeded by the dense bush, a sharp tangled net that I could not penetrate. Quite suddenly the finding stopped. But, my appetite whetted, I was now greedy for more evidence; I began to scratch around among the roots and chaff.

I thought of the native people of Waower Island, canoes hidden behind the high rock in the chasm; these others behind this bush tunnel in a small grove. But who was coming? The raiders from beyond the mist? The slave makers? Or the long arm of the law? Waower Island was a place of hiding. I backed out with none of my questions answered.

I found *Raven Moon* within inches of floating away. The tide had risen quickly to cover the thousand islets of tiny stones with their barnacle caps, perhaps one or two stone mauls and the lower part of the canoe runs.

I donned my anorak. I did not want to camp on Waower Island. I prepared for a cool rising late afternoon breeze to carry me safely away.

# 10.　Zen Beach

THE CRACKLING sound of fire from the direction of the beach told me morning had come. The drift of conversation in the air announced that my friends were up. Travelling with other kayakers in Barkley Sound had become routine. The friends I chose did not seem to mind my dawdling before the scenery, or my lingering with sketchbook and pen. They were artists themselves in their own way.

I dressed and hurried to the beach and the warm morning fire and conversation. "Camping would really be fun if the food weren't such tasteless muck," said Philip at the same moment I startled a marten who was stealing a package of butter and dragging it down between the logs.

"They don't think it's muck!" I shouted, running after the small mammal to save the camp rations. The martens were a well-fed lot here since mice, their principle tasteless muck, were abundant. At night we were often entertained by the sound of the tiny tenants of the island metropolis. Then suddenly all the playful skittering would stop and heavier footfalls could be heard in the dark. All life would be held in abeyance until at last the air would be rent with the fearful cries of a tiny victim. The mice never had a chance against predators five times their size. Within minutes of each

blood-chilling massacre the place would come alive with the scurrying of mice again. I would lie awake anguished by battles of life and death. "I'm definitely on the side of the mice," said Philip, as he dumped out half a cup of granola into the weeds at the edge of our camp.

Philip now announced that he wanted to solo for the day, which would give Mike, who would be coming out at the end of a day's work, a chance to catch up to us at Turret Island. He decked out his kayak and left for the outside coast. Len said he wanted to enjoy the island and would spend the day painting and meditating. I took *Raven Moon* and headed out to explore Willis, Dodd and the Brabant Islands.

My way lay through the gap between Tricket and the two Lovett Islands. There I found the water playing on the edge of a lot of large cobbles. I was not keen to embrace rocks in passing, so I rounded the top of the chain of the four sister islands, and let the following sea do the work of propelling me forward; all I had to do was brace as the waves rolled under the stern. It was a gentle roller coaster ride along the north beaches. In no time I had rounded nearby Willis Island and was soon ashore on a sandy, weedy beach.

Today solitude was my companion at Willis Island. My sketchbook sat idle on my lap as I indulged myself by

fetching water from the ferny spring and toasting my friends as I relived great old memories. The water became wine far sweeter than any I had imbibed in a long time.

One of the highlights of an earlier trip to the same area had been when Philip and I explored Lovett Island in fine detail. We had found it full of exciting surprises not noticeable from the water. Every tiny beach was made of cast up mussel shells and broken clams. The sun had come out of the mist to sizzle the shore edges. It was true that every beach was an individual with its own ragged rocks and twisted trees, and tiny deep tide pools with rounded boulders. Great purple sea urchins kept company with languorous anemones in those pools; they prickled along in their world like armoured samurai.

On the east corner of the small enchanting island, knotted trees had writhed from the tops of rocky turrets in a motion too slow to witness. Philip climbed the rocks and found the dinner table of predator birds and brought down their spiny bowl, a purple urchin, empty, husked. He wanted to take it home to his wife.

TIDE POOL

"I don't think it's meant to be crushed into a kayak with bedding and food," I said. "But since it doesn't look like rain is imminent, I can lend you my sou'wester to carry it in, if you like."

In the winter months that followed we sometimes met to discuss future trips. During my visits the urchin would be brought out and we would marvel over its size, its fragility, and the care with which my friend had brought it home packed in my sou'wester, the perfect-shaped case for it.

As I finished my cup of spring water, I blended back into the quietness of sitting on this beach by myself today. I retrieved my open page with the tiny islet and the rocks all made of ink, but my heart had drifted away into the land of memory. Perhaps the heady wine I had been drinking was turning me maudlin . . . I could draw no more.

I left Willis Island behind to her ghosts and paddled on, but thoughts of other more exciting trips made this one seem the less for its slow pace. All this changed when I returned to the swells along the north shores of the Lovetts. At the top of the two islands, I faced the rolling sea. It was a hard slog facing the swells. Now it was time to slip through the channel and head to our Turret Island base camp, but I was under the control of a different power and I did a strange thing; I suddenly turned, and catching a large wave, thrust *Raven Moon* around until we were facing the opposite direction. Caught by the waves behind me, I slid down their shoulders heading back the way I had come — and I was bracing hard just to keep on track. The lift and push behind me exhilarated some wild wish for excitement. My paddle blades flashed with light as I rolled along with the waves. In this new direction the sun sparkled along the shores ahead of me, dazzling, taunting. I picked up the pace through the force of sea under me. We sped past rocky ledges, past boulders, past trees, all in a mad race of flashing light.

Suddenly a shelf of white, untracked beach flashed into my sight. There was not a mark on it. At the water's edge large cobbles forbade a paddler to land. On either side high rocks covered in twisted trees prevented anyone's approach by foot. On a contorted limb I noticed an eagle sat watching.

I slowed down to take a better look, checked the wave pattern, waited for a lull, then I whipped out a grease pencil from my lifejacket pocket. I could not hold my sketchbook, but I could draw on the deck!

I held my paddle above the waves, checked the scene, drew and checked, drew and checked, then realized, as if it wasn't me who was there, how precarious my situation was. With the boat slowed almost to a stop and the paddle close to the deck, the force of the water could easily catch the flat surface of the paddle blades and flip me over — but drawing what I saw was worth the danger of a spill! At the moment I didn't care; the sea could have me! What difference did it

make to one small drop of nothing in this vast, incredible moment of beauty? I was blinded by the light, sat poised on the lip of Heaven! For a brief second the boat and my self dropped away. I became only the water, rising — subsiding — rising — subsiding, on the writing hand that moves and then moves on.

There's nothing more than this instant, I thought, no need to relive memories . . .

Lifted high again, the moment was over. I thrust the grease pencil into my pocket just in time as a wave grabbed the paddle. I touched down upon a hair's breadth of the point of no return. Desperately I sliced the paddle back out of the water, lifted it, grabbed it in both hands and swung into a shoulder-wrenching brace. More adrenalin — its waves seared my ribs.

When I looked up the little beach was gone.

All I had now was what lay on the deck, a few black wavering lines, but definitely, to me, the beach and the eagle. . .

The Zen beach has given me a koan, I realized, as I looked desperately for it once again and found it gone.

It was time for me to return to camp. I wasn't even sure

of the way back. Then I saw the two Lovetts and made my way to the gap between the islands. I found a new wind rising; white horses plunged far out, distant Sail Rock had a white skirt, and the roar of incoming weather grew loud.

I ran before the wind. But I no longer minded whatever the weather threw at me today. The play of the wind just made *Raven Moon* dance.

"What a great trip!" I shouted against the wind to Len as I struggled out of *Raven Moon*, my legs barely carrying me up the Turret Island beach.

Len looked up and held up a sketchbook with a swirl of colour. "It's Turret Island," he said. He had been caught by excitement of a different sort; painting was new to him.

A little later Philip returned, blown shoreward on a gust meant for him alone. Salt rime rimmed his eyebrows. Like the Ancient Mariner, he pointed a finger at far-off Sail Rock.

By late evening the white horses completely surrounded our island. We bunched close around our campfire and nursed mugs of hot cocoa within the halo of wild water. "We're in the eye of the storm," said Philip. "No one would even venture out to rescue us in this."

Len pulled a blanket round his shoulders and hunched up till the edges of it were almost touching the fire. Philip poked at embers with a stick, and sparks of light flashed upward and blew away.

I stared through the smoke and the sparks. The fire creased the men's faces into sardonic masks.

Suddenly, from behind a wall of surrounding logs, an apparition rose like a great lump of flotsam in the dark. It came toward us silently, dripping seaweed and water as it approached the fire.

Just before panic brought flight a voice said, "Can you tell me the way to Turret Island?"

It was not Mike. We had long given up expecting him to come out in the storm. This was Neptune paying us a visit; he bore no trident, but carried in one hand his paddle, in the other a drenched duffel bag from which he produced a bottle of Frangelico. To toast safe travel, he said, and for those in kayaks on the sea.

# 11.  Salal Joe's Garden

OVERHEAD BLACK clouds filled the sky and far-off thunder rattled the hills. It was obvious my latest Barkley Sound excursion was thwarted for now. *Raven Moon* sat in dry dock on the roof racks of my car, a nylon cover crimped tight like a chef's cap to the cockpit to keep out the rain. I huddled inside the car with my box of gear. If I could bear one night of such tight quarters, perhaps morning would be fine enough for me to leave shore with my camping gear still dry. My plan for this trip was to bestow upon Turret Island some seedlings of mint and cress that I had tucked away amongst my gear. I hoped to start a crop of herbs that I might harvest for salad and tea on future trips.

I collapsed the back seat of the Scirrocco and unrolled my sleeping bag. As I wormed my way inside, I could hear occasional rumblings of the thunder, but in a short time it seemed to have retreated to the slopes far away, while the mist moved silently past the hills looking for new valleys to haunt.

At least I was dry. I lay listening to the staccato of rain on the roof and on *Raven Moon*. Sleep did not come easily. I even thought about heading out in the unsettled weather. I felt strangely wide awake, energized, perhaps, by the ions in the air.

I tried to concentrate on Barkley Sound in the hope that

pleasant thoughts would have a soporific effect and lull me off to sleep. My mind drifted to a story a friend had told me about a reclusive man who had been a squatter in Barkley Sound. Salal Joe, as he was known, had been there when the islands had become part of Pacific Rim National Park in the 1970s and had been allowed to remain under the tradition of squatter's rights. Joe was a reaper of the branches of that plant's shiny green leaves, and an eater of the wild purple-black berries that grew on the southeastern sides of the islands in the Broken Group. He made the small income he required selling salal to the Vancouver Island florist shops.

Salal Joe lived on a floating raft and spent his time foraging among the islands in a small wooden dinghy. On Dodd Island he had established a quite remarkable garden. Not content just to grow essentials, Joe had planted not only a cherry tree, a plum tree and an apple tree, but also a rosebush, a mountain ash and a great clump of bamboo.

When the small island deer began to nibble off bits of tree bark and the roses from his bushes, he went off scrounging the beaches until he found some great fishnets. These he dragged home half in and half out of the dinghy, a job that must have taken days. Then he put up driftwood posts, secured the netting with bits of scrounged rope and made a gate out of beach-worn wood. At last he closed his garden to all save the insects and birds.

Salal Joe had an abiding love for the area and it must have been alarming to find the very first park visitors — and there were not many back then — come drifting up to his floathouse to ask directions or just to chat.

Joe became a well-known character to those who visited the area. And if they came back to the islands in another year, they would find he hadn't changed; he was just as peculiar as ever. Joe claimed he had escaped from Russia, where he was suspected of being a spy, and always added that he didn't mind. In fact, he would say, he was quite likely just going to disappear someday. He'd be gone to lie on the beaches soaking up the sun in California.

And then early one season an upturned boat was discovered banging against the logs on one of the islands at high tide. Closer investigation proved what the park superintendent had feared. It was Salal Joe's dinghy.

A search was instigated, starting at the floathouses on Turtle Island and continuing around Dodd Island. Here the gate to the garden was found swinging in the afternoon wind. That was unusual! Joe always kept the gate latched. Perhaps it was an oversight, but was there a connection? Had he hurried away from the garden for some reason? Had he got caught in one of those southwest winds? They often got up fast, in ten minutes, first with patches of gooseflesh on the water, and then calm again, and then the onslaught like a broom rushing down through the channels to sweep everything out toward the open sea.

After several days park officials really began to fear the worst, but a search of both high tides and low produced not a trace.

Did anyone know if Joe had been able to swim? Nobody could answer. No one wanted to accept the possibility that a sudden wind had swept him from his boat. They decided that Joe, true to his word, had gone off to the beaches of California. And so the search was stopped.

The floathouse remained a derelict. One of the park officials kindly latched up the garden gate, and with that latching, Joe faded into the folklore of the past.

My recollection of the Salal Joe story put me off to sleep at last. Though I tossed and turned several times during the night, I slept through and awoke with relief to find the mountains silent, clear and cloudless.

If only I had more time, I thought, during my three-day stay, perhaps I could have fitted in a stop on Dodd Island to look for Salal Joe's garden. But if I did that as a side trip, I would thwart my original plan to go around the outside coast and look for the cave on Dicebox Island.

Deciding to stick with my first intention, I set out directly to Turret Island. There I surveyed the local stream for a suitable planting spot for the mint and cress. It was disappointing to find the scene quite different than the image I had carried in my mind of a green wood and freckled sunlight. The place by the stream was brown and dark, the tall hemlocks oppressive. There was very little light, and the rapidly drying pools were covered in the oily scum so typical of centuries of piled-up conifer needles. It was unlikely that mint and cress would survive in such a place; my plan had been only the fantasy of a hungry winter mind. Nevertheless, I would plant some anyway, but save the best of the plants in the hope of finding a more suitable location. I rummaged in my boat, but found as I hunted high and low, muttering under my breath as I pulled out packet after packet of my food supplies until everything lay in a heap on the beach, that there was nothing resembling either mint or cress anywhere amongst my supplies. At last I came to the conclusion that my plant packages were still sitting on the steps at home where I had placed my gear ready for loading.

After three attempts to find the missing plants, I looked up to find that the rose and pink of morning had now levelled a finger of strong wind down the channels between the islands. It was not going to be the best weather for Dicebox Island after all. I could get trapped there, perhaps for days, by bad weather. Even Turret Island was too exposed. I must reorganize my trip plans. Within half an hour I had repacked my gear and was heading off to find a campsite on a more protected island.

As I paddled *Raven Moon* down the length of Turret Island the wind freshened, and I soon found myself in a losing battle to maintain my course. I flew past Turtle Island all in a rush. Was it the wind that turned my boat toward Dodd Island?

That's not a bad idea after all, I thought, and stopped fighting *Raven Moon* for control. Why not adapt to the second plan and go to see if I could find Salal Joe's garden?

*Raven Moon*, once she had her head, behaved like an unruly horse. She seemed to know full well of her capabilities in rough seas. As I backbraced just to keep her balanced, she nosed her way along and Dodd Island loomed up dead ahead. She took me straight ashore.

As soon as she nudged the beach, I leapt out and dragged her free of the dumping waves, up over the kelp and the drifted logs until she was securely above the tides. Stepping

back to breathe myself free of the exertion, I looked up to take my bearings. Directly above me was a square of boards and fishnets. Salal Joe's garden!

Thoughts of the open coast disappeared. I could find a more appropriate camping ground later, when the wind dropped. For now I wanted to see why Salal Joe had chosen this island over all the others for his garden.

Salal Joe had been missing now for four years, and I found the path he had made was rapidly disintegrating. New growth obliterated most of the early marks, but the imposing height of upended beach logs covered in plastic netting strangely had no look of decay about it at all.

Construction of this garrison must have been a monumental task, and the determination to create a safe spot for growing plants must have been of supreme importance for the man to have laboured with a fence so heavy and so permanent. It stood above my head by a good two feet. I could not see to the inside for the thickness of its layers against the boards, but I could see trees, trees that were nothing like the varieties found in the forest. These had large lacings of leaves that clattered together, making their own special music in the wind.

I approached the closed gate, hand outstretched. Then I remembered my friend's comment about the park officials who had found it unlatched and almost symbolically had done it up. It seemed a strange gesture, almost as if with the latching of a gate one could contain the essence of the strange man who had created the place, that maybe never would the inside of this garden decay so long as the outside was not let in.

A group of crows distracted my thoughts as they began cackling in the forest beside me. Were they sending me warnings? I looked up at them in the branches of the hemlocks above me and clicked my tongue noisily to make them flap off down the beach to continue their racket out of my way.

I realized suddenly that I had dropped the gate latch during the noisy intrusion. I quickly put out my hand. As I grasped it again the crows flew back to chide me once more. In a moment of irritation I decided to ignore them; I would see the garden whether the crows or the gate approved or not. Taking hold of the latch, I pushed against a resistant layer of grass. With a creaking of old bones it yielded to my strength. I took a step into another world . . .

You could tell the place had once burgeoned and blossomed. Everything had grown in a crazy, rampant way. There was the cherry tree, the mountain ash, the plum and the apple tree, and in one corner beside a clump of strange-looking bamboo, a rose had straggled over and become bound with creeping wild vines. The whole garden had a weedy growth wrapping it round in a wild tangle. The precious plants of Salal Joe had struggled hard for territory and existence. Without his care the years had taken a sad toll; many had strangled. Yet there was a mystique about the garden, a reverence that was part of the air within it. I found I wanted to sit down in spite of the mosquitoes that rose up from the long grass to feast upon any exposed flesh they could find. I wanted to sit, and as the artist Gauguin had said about art as abstraction, *derive the abstraction from Nature while dreaming before it*.

I chose a spot under the cherry tree, leaned my back against its trunk and for only a moment closed my eyes. It was good to rest after the toil of the morning in a place where the wind seemed absent. I felt my tired body relax; a deep peace began settling into my bones . . .

Suddenly my body gave a twitch. I opened my eyes and found myself staring at a huge forest slug as big as a cigar. I could see the slug's eyes out on stalks that moved up and down, this way and that, as if feeling the air while it oozed its way up the stem of the rosebush, looking for decayed matter to eat. All around the slug were the skeletons of eaten leaves.

Other bugs came into my vision, too, now that I was sitting still, slugs and centipedes. I sat quietly watching them munching away at the tender shoots of plants that were not natives of the place but had been brought there by loving hands to grow in the peace of the forested island. They had taken on an air of the exotic, a culinary specialty in the world of insects.

I suddenly felt vaguely uneasy. The peace and tranquillity that had overtaken me disappeared as quickly as they had come. Somewhere nearby the crows resumed their clattering cacophony.

I got to my feet, uncomfortable now, and hurried out of the garden. In a moment of respect for Salal Joe, I heaved the gate shut as I passed.

The crows flapped away in alarm. I ran down onto the beach, a strong feeling of apprehension hot on my heels, though I didn't know why. What time was it? To my horror I discovered the tide had come in while I was gone. And there was no sign of *Raven Moon*!

Frantic, I ran to the point of land that jutted from the corner of the island. How long had I slept? There was no sign of my kayak anywhere. I ran along the beach to the first point, then crossed the isthmus and back. I ran the other way until steep rocks stopped my passage. Anguish pushed all my blood to my brain. What was I to do now? I slumped down in a lump on the beach stones and shed tears of abject frustration. What now?

It was some time before the first glimmerings of reason began to filter back. I could wait it out; perhaps someone would come by, another kayaker, boaters perhaps. But this was only May, I realized. I had deliberately chosen to come out of season when there was unlikely to be another soul in the area. I looked out to sea. The distant specks along the horizon were only islands and more islands, each wild and lonely and covered in trees. I had become the only human on earth and ocean.

I walked dejectedly back across the shore. At least I had taken my gear out of the boat. At least I had done that; but I bitterly regretted not having realized that *Raven Moon* was my only lifeline to civilization. I had been careless. I had not secured her. She had been intractable all day, and now she was gone.

There was little I could do about it, so I occupied myself with setting up my tent. With the food I had brought I would be comfortable for several days before hunger became a serious threat. There would, of course, be seafood after that, so I would not starve. Water, though, might pose a different problem. In my canteen I had only enough, if rationed, for three or four days at most. Zipped inside my tent, I could light the little candle for the dark. It might last two days — some comfort . . .

But what about *Raven Moon*? I counted out the approximate hours till tide change, knowing with incredible hindsight that I hadn't even brought the tide book for local waters, only my charts. What were my chances of finding

*Raven Moon* further around the island as soon as the next low tide allowed me to get along the beach? It was a glimmer of hope — perhaps she had only drifted a beach or two away. After all, she had wanted to come here in the first place, hadn't she? What were my chances the next rising tide might just wash her back to this same beach? Now that's too much, I thought — a chance that was less than remote. I cursed myself for not having brought a flashlight so that I could search if the tide went out during the night. Most of all, I cursed *Raven Moon* for her betrayal.

With one of thirteen matches I built a roaring fire and got out my camp billy, thinking that food would cheer me up. Inside my cooking pot when I opened it were some Ziploc bags. Inside these were the packages of cress and mint that I thought I had left at home in Deep Cove. They had been with me all along!

I quickly opened the bag so the plants could breathe and then set about making a big stew in the pot. After dinner I would do something about them. Finding the plants made me feel much more cheerful. Maybe I wasn't so stupid after all. I would buck up and do the best I could.

I sat down to my repast, but, as I poked down mouthfuls that tasted like paper, I couldn't help thinking of my treasured boat being salvaged on distant shores by callous mariners.

When my plate was empty I set about searching for trails that might lead to the hidden beaches of the island. The first one I found led through high patches of salal, which I pushed out of my way as I went, noting that at some time long ago there had been a well-cut path. Suddenly I was out on the beach again. The island had an unexpectedly narrow isthmus hidden by dense groves of salal. Down the beach was a small lagoon and what looked like a freshwater stream.

No wonder Salal Joe had liked this island! It was simply beautiful in the real sense: a horseshoe bay of small cobblestones, driftwood whitened by long exposure to the sun along the half circle, marsh grass hedging the banks of the purling brown stream that spilled out of the bush and snaked its way to sea. Windfallen trees crossed the narrow inlet in three or four places, making it possible for me to cross back and forth over the stream. I tasted the water above the beach and found it was fresh and sweet. I began to look for a grassy pocket of growing soil; it was time to plant the mint and cress.

Returning quickly to my camp, I fetched the bags with their green and precious cargo, then kneeling down, a little like a suppliant at prayer for my good fortune at being still well and safe on shore, I cupped my hands and pulled up in each a lump of the peat-like earth, tucked in the plant shoots and tamped them down.

Overhead, crows moved silently into my awareness again. They had stopped scolding, but I felt they were keeping an eye on me with concentrated curiosity. I caught glimpses of their iridescent black shadow shapes drifting from limb to limb above me. I wondered if they carried some of the essence of the legendary gardener of Dodd Island.

Now that I had completed my chore, I suddenly felt a lightened mood. It wasn't so bad to be a castaway. I thought of Robinson Crusoe. This might have been a choice place to live. There were berries and green food. There was water, and there was the garden.

I soon shrugged it off. It's crazy, I thought. I can want this kind of life a lot, but circumstance has already given me a very different script. I am an artist, and I need the stimulation of life near a village with other people around, with libraries, bookstores, at least for part of the year. It was madness even to entertain the thought that I might be happy spending all my time on a quiet little island with ravens and crows — but what was it that Salal Joe threw away in favour of the hermit life? I kept asking myself.

It grew dark while I pondered the mystery of the strange inhabitant. The crows went to roost for the night. They totally accepted their life here on the island, while I continued to think of all that was valuable in the choice I had made when I bought land in Deep Cove.

I decided not to worry, not yet; a boat would come eventually. My house sitter, after waiting an extra day or two for the chance of bad weather making it impossible for me to be on time, would send out the alarm.

I returned to my tent just before it was too dark to see. There I packed everything for the night. I made one last desperate check of the beach in a vain hope of recovering my recalcitrant boat. Then I lit my candle and crawled inside the tent and into my night attire, first my woolies, then my sleeping bag. This would not be a bad life, I told myself again as I warmed up in the comfort of the nest I had made.

I'm not sure when in the night Salal Joe made his appearance, but I somehow knew that he would come. I had long been told that creatures from the spirit world would not harm me. I had made the decision not to sit up wasting rationed midnight wax to keep a ghost away.

First there was much crackling of the dry mossy undergrowth near my tent; then I heard footfalls too loud for mice. Though I never lifted the tent flap, I began to see him standing outside. I noticed suddenly that he was reaching out toward me, that he held something in his hand. Something that glinted in the moonlight now speckling among the trees. A shiny object. I stared out through the mosquito netting. Yes, it was a stick, old, shiny with hand rubbing — a digging stick like the Indians used.

A hot feeling speared down through the centre of me. Salal Joe actually wanted me to take the stick; he kept reaching out with it. I pulled a trembling hand from the warmth of the sleeping bag and, removing the mosquito curtain that stood between us, I reached and took the smooth old stick from the cold night air.

At once the apparition vanished. I stared out at the low slung cedar branches moving gently in the breath of the night . . .

There was no breeze in the morning. It was quiet and still; mist moved softly over the water. I prepared my granola, but did not have the usual enthusiasm for camp food. I knew I should have felt at ease and glad that morning had come, that things were getting warm, but a vague uneasiness rattled me. It was as if there were something I had left undone.

I recalled the dream — but it hadn't been a dream! I had been wide awake when the bushes had crackled. I had seen

the strange man at my tent door. Even the mice had stopped scuttling when the apparition had visited camp. And he had brought me something, had handed it to me before I had scared him away.

I put down my food and hurried to the tent. I fumbled around the sides of my sleeping bag. Yes, there it was — a digging stick, like the Indians used. That was it! Of course!

I left the breakfast I was eating for the mice to enjoy; I had had enough. There was so much to do today! I hurried over to the fishnet and log fence. Quickly I undid the gate latch and entered the garden.

Hours passed. My hands turned black from the rich midden soil as I set to weeding and clearing out the choking roots that had overtaken the garden plot. When at last I knelt up from my toil, all that survived of Salal Joe's plants were clear of weeds, even the rosebush. And as if to reward me, I discovered buds on it that had been hidden by stifling wild vines. It would bloom now. That must have been what Salal Joe had wanted, to see the garden blossom . . .

The job done, I knelt back and looked up above the high netting into the hemlock trees. Then I caught a glimpse through the fishnet mesh of the jungle of salal pressing ever closer toward the fence as time went by. I saw the small flock of island crows watching me quizzically from low-hanging branches.

"There, it's done," I said aloud, knowing suddenly as I said it that I was now free from the spell of the island. The crows stared back at me, not making their usual racket, but staring silently.

I stood up and once more admired Salal Joe's wonderful garden. Yes, I thought, one could live here alright. Living this way would have all kinds of rewards. I backed out of the garden very quietly and latched the gate behind me. The crows went off down the beach to hunt for clams.

It was time to go. I looked down the shore and smiled at *Raven Moon* where she rested on the mark of the high tide.

# 12.    Cape Scott Real Estate

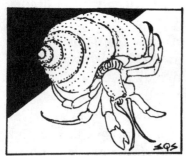 CIVILIZATION WAS encroaching on my home territory of Deep Cove. The world had discovered paradise and had come flocking into the area to live. The more this happened, the more I was driven to move outward in my search for the out-of-the-way places. As well as kayaking, I began hiking as a way of escaping the crowd. An incident that happened on a trek to Cape Scott with a friend brought home to me the state of land development and its effect upon me.

Cape Scott was one place that would not hear the roar of bulldozers, followed by lawnmowers and barbecues on sundecks, not for a while, I thought, as we stood on a wide crescent of beach at the north end of Vancouver Island.

"If I could only buy a place up here," sighed Mary, as she looked both ways along a silver horseshoe of surf and sand.

"It's the development where I live," I said. "That's what really bothers me!" Above us was a solid margin of trees that hemmed the sand of Cape Scott. I saw the contrast in my mind's eye: in place of the forest, a wall of houses.

"The developers take out the trees and they blow up the rocks and then they sell them," said Mary. "I don't understand it."

"There's money to be had in trees and rock, that's part of the problem," I said. "And nowadays land can be rearranged

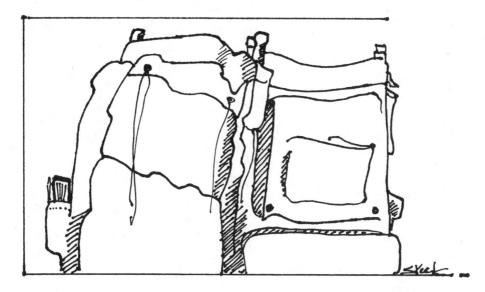

to suit anyone's desires. They just take it out of Nature's hands. Country life has become street lights and sidewalks and everyone wants to live in paradise."

Mary looked away at the ocean. "It's better to be a nomad — own nothing."

I was beginning to like hiking with Mary. We had met by chance in a camping supply store and had recognized one another as canoe club members. When Mary suggested we take a trip together and then added, "But I do like elbow room; we'll have to take our own tents," I realized we would not be following too close in one another's footsteps. I accepted.

Within two weeks we were on the trail, a rough bog-ridden course of swamps and pole bridges, snags and hollows. We had fallen when bush pushed us off the bridges, and our hiking poles had sometimes sunk to the hilt in quagmire as we tested our course.

When Mary and I came to the meadow, she called them the fields of history and recounted some of their story.

Rasmus Hansen had discovered the field after going ashore from a sailing vessel to hunt. He decided to apply to the government to start a township and bring out his kinsmen from Denmark to colonize the remote north end of the island. He applied to the government for roads and land grants.

Within five years a surprising ninety families had arrived to colonize Cape Scott. Then there was a change in office. The promise of roads and land purchase was suddenly withdrawn. The settlers found themselves cut off. They continued to attract colonists, continued to receive some supplies by ship, although there were no suitable landings because the coastline was full of shallows, high surf and seven miles of reefs offshore.

By the 1930s most of the families had disappeared back into the rest of the world, leaving Cape Scott and its golden fields to return to wilderness once more.

It was the traces of what remained that had piqued Mary's interest. "They dyked the field," she said, "and while the settlers were celebrating in the new community hall, the dyke spoiled its own inauguration ceremonies. The sea broke through. What a study in futility."

We stood looking over the clones of the same golden grass that, full of false promise, had waved in the wind before Hansen. Under the grass we found a mire that sucked and seeped to liquid oblivion. It was no good to build dreams on sand, I said.

Above the tides on the bight we put up a plastic rain and wind shelter using plentiful beach trash and salvaged rope. Beside this we erected our tents, with a distance of thirty feet between. In an hour's time we had become temporary squatters on the land, each with her own beach domain, each strongly maintaining her independence.

The following morning I began sketches of the scenery around camp while Mary went off along the sands. I was beginning to relax; thoughts of land development were fading away into a glorious landscape of wide open beach.

Mary and I were not making footsteps in each other's tracks. She disappeared in the morning. When she came back, she told me excitedly that she had found a suitable bathing pool in the low tide rocks two miles along the shore. Baths in this part of the world, she thought, would be scarce. I looked down at the rime of trail mud that had lingered like a high-tide line around my knees and noticed that her legs were clean.

The low fog layers of the August morning eased past our

camp and burned off with the hours, leaving a summer
afternoon and a warming beach of clear delineation. Water on
the sand refracted the light through the trees and reversed
their image before me as I walked along toward the baths in a
magic web of dark green on the background blue of a damp
sky. The sun danced ahead of me between cloud cracks.
Stopping, I watched transfixed as the shattered water image
resettled around my feet. It was like walking in my own
painting. In those moments I understood the need to keep
paradise free from man's development even more clearly than
ever. I was in the middle of a silent wilderness — no
hammers, no bulldozers, no dynamite, just the roar of surf,
just the sounds of nature. But I also knew that mankind was a
rapidly proliferating species that needed a place — would I
deny a home for my own children?

When I reached the rocks Mary had described I selected
the largest of several pools and stripped down until I was
shivering in the cool ocean breeze. I gasped as I slid in among
imagined icicles and briskly began washing with the tiny
square of cloth I had torn from my paint rag especially for the
occasion. Mary and I had laughed about it when I had rinsed
out the last traces of colour from the rag and had told her my
plan. Her comment was: only a serious artist would wash

with a paint rag for a face cloth. I began vigorously and soaplessly to lave away a lot of my heavy thoughts on mankind's arrival in what I innocently had thought would remain my private paradise. I used my paint rag to remind myself that I mustn't bog down in the weight of life's problems, but keep a light heart — be an artist. I wrung the paint rag out and dried myself as best I could, then I sat on the rocks and let the sun do the rest.

The satin soft feeling and protection of clothes followed the icy embrace. Gone was the web of grime that had accumulated.

Ensconced on the rock, I removed my sketchbook from my daypack at the same time that I noticed the second pool. Unlike the pool I had disturbed, the new one seemed to be vibrant with life, with hermit crabs scuttling about in a frenzy of activity. It's like the heart of the world where I live, I thought, as I moved closer and squatted down on my heels like a voyeur. My pen was poised on the lip of a world in microcosm, I told myself. At first I thought the hermit crabs were being very affectionate. Then I realized I was witnessing a wrestling match, not a love-in. The creatures were stressful, seemed overwrought. I leaned even further over, peering intently into the pool. It was some moments before I began to understand the reason for the crabs' distress. Hermit crabs do not have their own shells; they live in the cast-offs of other crabs and snails. The creatures were engrossed in trying to expropriate each other's homes.

Perhaps I could help, I thought, and got up to walk in circles, searching the sand for empty shells so that I could join in with the fun. I soon realized there was nothing on the exposed beach — the violence of the surf had left no shells intact. Then I remembered that last evening I had retrieved a small colourful snail shell from the sand near our camp when we had arrived; I had put it into my pocket as a memento. I now pulled it out, but I found to my surprise and regret that there was an occupant closed tight within the tiny chamber inside. Unwittingly, I had imprisoned a little wizened crab in the confines of my dry, dark pocket. The best thing I could do now was to try to revive it by setting it free. I climbed

back to the pool and dropped it in. My folly became instantly apparent. Several of the largest hermit crabs set upon the shell, viciously yanking out the poor comatose inmate and abandoning it to its fate on the bottom of the pool. It wasn't food they wanted, only the empty shell. In a lightning-swift movement the largest hermit leapt from its own shell and sequestered its naked and vulnerable rear end into the new one. Its own shell fell to the pond floor. Instantly there was another scuffle and a repetition of the first transaction. A chain reaction followed; tenants shifted and moved. It all happened so swiftly that I soon lost track of which home was going on the market. Every abandoned house was squabbled and fought over in vicious crab tug-o-wars. The last I saw, a tiny periwinkle shell, too small to be of use, was the only place left up for grabs. It was being fought over by crabs who couldn't possibly squeeze inside. In the world of hermit crabs, I realized, a vacant house would soon be swept away. One had to secure one's home before the deadlines of the tides. Meanwhile, a large crab of another variety, whose own house was firmly secured permanently to his back, took the body of the deceased pocket occupant and ate it behind the rocks, out of sight of anyone who might want to share.

Was I seeing the world's problems in a nutshell I asked myself? No — in a hermit shell . . .

I spent an intriguing afternoon by the pool and returned to base camp as the sun was settling into the sea. Sandbars turned gold, then pink. The light wind chilled my face, and the cool blue of night chased the other colours away. I saw my tent shining in the half-light, a welcome residence. But through my head, uncomfortably, there flashed an image of Mary, a person I barely knew and yet had agreed to camp with, taking my tent for her own while I was gone so long, leaving me to search the beach for another place to shelter me for the night. I shivered with apprehension as I walked that night on the shifting sand in a world of villainous real estate.

# 13.　Spirit Essence

"WHAT BROUGHT you to Cape Scott?" asked Mary one grey morning. "You don't seem to be all that interested in the settlers, not the way I am, so what is it?"

"Oh, it's wolves," I said.

Wolves had slipped out first before the other reasons, reasons like my wanting to write a journal, and sketch wilderness, and live in a tent again, wanting to explore the top of Vancouver Island, reasons like the scenery, the settlers, the sea, and most of all to get away from the changing landscape at home. I had decided at the time to keep quiet about painting. I hadn't wanted to put Mary off with some idea that I might spend hours on the beach sitting in one spot while I slaved away putting the metaphorical oil on canvas as she stood around shifting from one foot to the other. Some people, I knew, had funny ideas about artists.

"Wolves," I said again.

Knee-deep along the tideline lay great roils of kelp, leftovers of a recent storm. Along this line sandpipers pounced the edge, turning the sheeted sand to lace with their tiny feet and beaks as they searched for food. Gulls postured and stomped on top of the mounds. None of them paid any attention to the one lone bird that was struggling in the breakers. Each time a wave wiped it away from shore, the next one would sweep it back again. I ran over and snatched the victim from the sea's cruel game.

"What are you doing?" asked Mary.

"I don't know, but the sea's not going to have this bird! It's going to die." We gathered round.

"What can we do? Nothing," said Mary, answering her own question.

"Nature has no time for losers," I sighed. "Perhaps we can put it in the stream below our camp. We can't get it out beyond the surf where it needs to be. I've saved birds before," I added, brightening. "A year ago I saved a grebe when it got marooned on the roadside. I was travelling by in my car — after midnight — when I saw it. I went home for a fishnet, caught the bird, and took it down onto the beach."

"What was wrong with it?"

"It had landed on the pavement and couldn't get airborne. Grebes need water to take off on; you know how they run along the surface of the water to get up? When I set it free it circled the beach making such plaintive cries; I guess it was searching for others of its kind in the dark. I'll never forget the sound. I used to bring home the starved, the sick and the frozen, ever since I can remember, and often with tragic results, but sometimes things lived and that would make it worth it. Why don't we take the murrelet to the stream?" I suggested.

The bird lay with its head in the water. Mary scavenged an old milk crate and we carried the bird to camp. "At least it can die out of the cold wind," she said.

At bedtime I took the remains of the murrelet to the high tideline and left it on the top of a large coil of kelp. "It can become food for the living," I said. "I just don't believe in burial when it can be food for other life."

This small chore done, we silently straightened our tents for the night and boiled water for tea.

"How about wolves tomorrow?" I asked as I departed for my tent. "It would be great if they would follow us along the sand. An acquaintance of mine said the wolves up here once followed him along the beach. They were great company, he said."

"You must be weird," said Mary. "I only want to see them in the distance."

"The best time would be early in the morning. I've never seen the wild ones; when I do see them, I'll know I'm in true wilderness — that's what wolves represent to me, the essence of real nature."

Wolf morning dawned clear, but soon drowned its false prophecy in a wall of mist. We rose in the dark and hurried along the beach toward its remote eastern end. I carried with me two oranges, my sketchbook and pen. If we were there in time, I thought, we might see them.

It began to drizzle as the fog filtered out the blue sky. Patting large drops warned us of a coming downpour. Mary and I huddled up against the beach drift, under huge logs as grey as the morning. I sketched silently. Mary sat watching.

Would the wolves come?

Time went by. We began to shiver with sitting still. The beach was awash now in steady, pelting rain. I pocketed my

waterproof sketchbook and my hands, too, after pulling my toque down to touch my eyebrows.

Mary whispered, "We must be crazy. Who but us would freeze to death or get soaked to the skin waiting for the chance just to see a wolf?"

We consumed our oranges to cheer ourselves up and buried the peel by digging holes with our boot heels rather than getting our hands covered in clinging wet sand. Silence was all around and the tide far out. We looked down the beach at the heavy clouds and the fog that paraded past. The rain stopped. All was distant waves and sand, grey drift logs and silence.

At last we could abide it no more. "Let's go back."

I put away my drawings. Hunger prompted us in the direction of a campfire and more substantial food. We trudged back in a slow procession toward the south end of the beach.

By our camp we saw the tracks. As large as those of big dogs they embroidered the beach before us in a wild weaving, over the logs, along the sand, the pattern broken only around the spot where I had placed the dead murrelet. Here the footprints came together in a tight knot to surround

a scratch mark where there had been a confrontation over who would eat the tiny corpse and who would not.

Wolves!

Like spirits, they had come and gone in the earliest part of the morning. We hadn't seen and we hadn't heard.

"If I hadn't gone to search for them," I said later. "If we'd only stayed in camp!"

As I was busy drawing the shadows of wolf spirits, the mist closed in and rain began to pelt once more. The patch of fog had followed us from the northern beach. The fresh downpour quickly obliterated the sharp edges of the exciting beach graffiti. If I'd waited in camp! I was left with only the wild spirit essence lingering in the morning air, traces of mist in the shape of wolves.

# 14.  Treasures

BEYOND OUR camp at Nels Bight we found open sand beaches and rugged, impassable rocky headlands. Rotting plank walks through dense groves of salal pointed the way to the lighthouse on the northwest tip of the island. The trails to and from the beaches had been brightly marked by passersby with old fishing floats, ropes and drifted bleach bottles.

Mary walked on the lower beach. I chose to walk on a steep bank of gravel in the hope of finding sketching material where the evergreens leaned over to form dark patches against the light grey stones. Under my feet I found a fossil, a strange whorled creature of another time. I called Mary before the ammonite went into my pocket.

"Don't forget how heavy your pack was coming in," she said.

I found a whalebone and I didn't call her. I sat and sketched it, while she went back to the lower beach. Then I measured the bone. It was three quarters the length of my hiking pole. Looking to see if Mary was watching, I tried to lift it, but it was too heavy, waterlogged. Pure Inuit art, I thought, marvelling, as I sat down to render the shape into my sketchbook.

Mary's daughter, Theresa, and her friend, Demi, who had

surprised me by joining us to camp at the Cape, came hiking by. "What are you going to do with it?" they said.

"I shall take it home," I lied; my thoughts were on Mary's comment. The girls walked off in a mist of laughter. "I'll tie it on my pack," I called out. Then, alone, I sat with my sketch.

In the undisturbed quiet, the Inuit archetypes peered out of the bone. The whales were migrants along this coast, I rationalized; they brought art down from the Arctic. Once in the Queen Charlotte Islands long ago, I remembered, I had discovered beach stones with worn underlayers whose centres were the perfect shape of the eyes depicted in Haida art. Art comes to artists through osmosis, I said to myself; it registers on the subconscious, then surfaces when we truly translate from our hearts what we see. Art becomes regionalized without the artist himself even knowing it. That's why the art that comes from British Columbia is unique, its rocks and bent trees, a place of challenge, a place of changing light. Perhaps staying in one place could work for an artist if he did not clutter his regionality by concentrating on other places as I often did, thinking about spreading outwards in a ripple effect to see the rest of the world. Remaining steeped in local idiom perhaps was the best of ideas; a person's art expression would belong to his own area of reference. Perhaps it could work for me, for it was becoming obvious that on an artist's budget, I would not travel away into other geography. I suddenly felt glad to have lived all of my life on Vancouver Island. I was rich in the circumstances of where I was born. Here at the edge of the Pacific Ocean, in these moments beside the whalebone, it crossed my thoughts that I should remain forever in the Vancouver Island wilderness.

So where are you going? I asked of the Inuit loon with its outspread wings. We'd both been dreaming, and the loon seemed about to take flight, to migrate like the whale it had come from. I hurried to bring the image out of the bone and onto the paper before things changed.

If I had been Inuit, I might just carve one or two lines into that bone and what was already there, once it had eyes, would look back. Then, if I were an artist, the thing would come alive. Hokusai again . . .

When I looked up, Mary was gone from the beach, and so were Theresa and Demi. I wasn't sure how long I had been an anchor while things around me took flight. I pushed my sketch into my lunch pack and picked up my pole. I left Loon where it was, drying its bone wings briefly in seaborne currents of air.

I followed the flotsam trail and the sandy footprints of my new friends up off the beach without looking back. I began climbing a hill trail over a log boardwalk that skirted a rocky headland. At the summit I found Mary, standing looking down over the screed slopes. "It's truly beautiful," she said. She was pointing to the surf-blanched rocks where the light was being played against the craggy shore by the motion of the waves. The rocks were outlined through the deep rich green of trees and the contrasting damp trunks and branches. Light hemmed the edges of things in aerated water, forever moving and alive. We stood for several moments surveying the wild coast of British Columbia, then as I put down my daypack Mary picked hers up; I noticed as she walked off that mine did not hang slack like hers did.

"I want to reach the girls at the Sandneck," she said as she disappeared down the hill.

I merely want to reach understanding — on the slow route, I said to myself, as I looked over the scree and my mind flashed back to the bone loon. "No need to hurry on," I called out to the silence. "I'll try to catch up," I called after Mary, and then I was alone in a vast expanse; I took out my sketching things again.

Her voice funnelled up through the trees, "Don't bring it all . . . "

Huge chunks of an old shipwreck lined the shore. The ship had been broken in three and drowned in the gravel of the bay.

"What ship is this?" I asked, knowing that Mary had done a lot of research.

"It's a barquentine, called the *Tolmie*, and it was towed here," said Mary. "It was built in Victoria, sailed to Africa and back and was finally brought here to make a breakwater, but storms broke it loose and cast it up onto the shore. Some breakwater. It must have been a shock to see what could happen here when the wind was wrong. The Danish people certainly had found out when they tried to make this place their port because Hansen's Lagoon was too shallow. It never worked.

"There's almost no reminder now of settlers," I said. "In spite of the fact that things preserved by a salt wind should last and last."

"Before the settlers this was a halibut ground," Mary went on. "Then Hansen, the original founder of the Cape Scott colony, and another Dane, named Nelsen, moved in. They built a home of driftwood. Then Hansen set off for Seattle on business, leaving Nelsen to winter alone here. Talk about isolation! Nelsen must have been an expert on that.

"When Hansen came back he was the new owner of the *Floyberg*, the schooner that had first brought him ashore the day he wandered up into the fields and dreamed his dream of starting a colony.

"When the *Floyberg* arrived, there were five good mariners on board with him, new settlers for the Cape. Because of big swells they couldn't land; the anchor wouldn't hold. They had to cut it free and go around the top of the island through seven miles of reefs, then they drove her anchorless onto the sand at Hansen's Lagoon, where the dykes were. The boat was wrecked. What an omen of disaster! The colony of Cape Scott was nothing but a hopeless dream."

I looked out onto the curve of trackless shore, a beach lying still in the sun of the present day, on an old wooden dinosaur with a broken back that now lay buried in gravel with alder trees on its topsides making new masts for its shore-going travels, nothing more.

I walked off, leaving Mary poking about the old ship's

structure. When I saw the strange tree at the top of the beach, I called her over. "I don't think this is a native of British Columbia," I said.

"That's the clearest artifact we've seen yet on this beach," said Mary. "It proves that people lived here — planned to live here. Garden trees get planted only by people who plan to stay a while."

We looked at the tree's strange knots and dense, compacted growth. Its survival in a tangle of heavy bush overshadowed by tall conifers seemed a miracle. "Better than the settlers," said Mary. "They lasted only thirty years in a hostile climate. I bet there was a house in here, too." She poked with her hiking pole, tapped at a crumbling plank, then pushed further into bush tangle.

I stayed on the fringes, trying to draw the special tree, to make it different — Danish. I soon gave up, while the bank invited me to rest and relax. "Isn't it lunchtime yet?" I called into the shrubbery.

"It must be," she said, coming out. She had sticks in her hair, but her eyes sparkled. She dove into her pack and came out

with cheese and a fistful of crackers. I took my time creating a sandwich with pita bread and peanut butter and sprouts I had grown in a bottle in my sleeping bag's warmth. "I don't know why you bring so much food," Mary said, as she watched my performance. She had finished eating and I'd not started.

"I need energy for lugging my heavy pack," I mumbled.

"Well, that makes sense," she said, with a look of scorn for my sandwich.

Did I need to make excuses? We were so different in many ways. I remembered how Mary had already made it plain that she hated miso, which was one of my staples. She thought my appetite and style of cookery were disgusting, had told me my food was some sort of Oriental unpalatable stuff and wouldn't touch it.

We derided one another for several moments on our quirks in diet, then laughed at ourselves. The best part about camping together, we were finding, was our ability to make buffoons of ourselves. We plucked a unanimously popular dessert of fresh thimbleberries from the bushes that lined Fisherman Bay.

"We could be eating the very food that sustained the

early colonists through their trials and travesties," said Mary, as she plucked handful after handful of the ripe fruit. We were immersed, with our arms reaching and reaching for the red thimbles when the beach intruder slipped out of the shadows of the old wreck. "Oh, no!" muttered Mary, with a tone in her voice that brought me backing up out of the bush with alacrity. The bear was well on his way toward us, nose twitching.

"This is no place to start an argument with a bear!" Mary shouted, as she grabbed up her pack and began scrambling into its tangle of straps. We quickly donated the berry patch to the wildlife and slipped into the forest.

On the map, it was only a short hike to cross the point to Nissen Bight where we would meet the girls. It turned out to be fraught with ups and downs over windfalls; I stopped to rest when I saw a clump of red polypores. "I'm taking these for dyeing silk," I said, as I struggled to bend with my pack on my back. I came up with a handful before I noticed that my hands were now bright red with polypore stain. "Macbeth," I said, trying to wipe off the dye on a mossy tree. Mary looked unimpressed. "Stained by the blood of the forest. What have I done?" I went on.

"Punishment," said Mary, "for desecrating the wilderness."

"You're saying I ought to be more environmentally conscious," I said. "Really I was only helping Nature do her pruning."

"What amazes me is the amount of treasures you bring home," she went on.

"We can't leave everything to the salt wind," I said. "We have to keep it in the present day. Our moments blow away with time," I said, full of drama. "Rust with the salt wind. Is there any harm in keeping small mementos?"

We went back to the high uncut wall of salal and fallen trees. Mary thrust her pack onto one of the supine trunks and scrambled up. As she did so, something fell out of the side pocket — a wooden peg. I retrieved it and handed it up to her.

There was a long pause, then, "Couldn't leave it," she said. "They don't make ships with wooden pegs anymore." A warm smile of recognition flashed in her eyes.

# 15.   Sandneck

"DON'T WE go left?" I asked, as rain blew sideways into my open mouth.

Mary laughed. "No, to the right."

"Surely not," I called out into the wind. "See? On the last beach the ocean was over our right shoulder. Now it's on the left. You only think you know the way."

Mary laughed again. "You should have looked at the map," she said. "It's a panhandle. You'll see when we come to the sandneck; there'll be ocean on the left as well as on the right."

I looked up at the narrow collar of dunes to which she pointed. I could see that it was only a band of unstable sand that joined the Cape Scott lighthouse rocks to mainland Vancouver Island, a mere few threads that looked as if they might blow away in the first storm. Over the top of the band was a ragged wind-blasted drift fence. "That's Jensen's," said Mary. "He was one of the first settlers."

"What was he keeping out?"

"He was keeping in — not out — clover, and cattle, and sand, keeping the turf from blowing away."

"And these tracks?"

"That's a plank road that was built by the army in the 1940s for the radar station."

"It's disorienting, this uneven ground," I said, as we struggled through the soft underfooting. Trees were sand-blasted with bare arms and pointed fingers. "Disquieting. It makes me feel uncomfortable — something deeper than the settlers and the army."

"It is a strange place," Mary answered. "Trees all drowned in sand."

"Disorienting," I reiterated.

Theresa and Demi disappeared over a pyramid taking their voices with them. I felt the rain pelt down and pit the ground around us. The sea was hidden from view. Something electric lifted the hairs on my arms as it would lift the thin blond grasses of the dune fields. What was causing it I didn't know. Perhaps a good few bites of food would take away the blinding lightheadedness. "Isn't it lunchtime?" I asked.

"You're always hungry," said Mary. We chose a sliding bank and dug into our wringing-wet bags to bring out our repasts. As I removed my sandwich bite by bite, my eyes were taking in the rain, wet broken shells and red firestones. I watched Theresa as water dripped from her hair and plastered it to her face. Demi stopped eating to pick up a white snail shell and brush the sand and rain from it. She was looking at it — more than just looking, I thought; she was absorbing it. It went into her pocket.

Lunch over, all of us disbanded in different directions. I went in search of my orientation, but as I combed the dunes, the eerie feeling went with me. I began to notice bones, fragments of them, broken and white, scattered among the strange bleached shells of snails that were replicas of the one Demi was carrying in her pocket.

I walked in a circle around the patch of snails, bones and stones. Once I caught sight of the girls as they drifted over the top of a dune nearby and, ghostlike, disappeared — an Andrew Wyeth painting, I thought. They seemed to drift weightlessly. Wyeth would have loved the tiny shell in Demi's pocket . . .

I tried sketching in the hope it would settle the uneasy

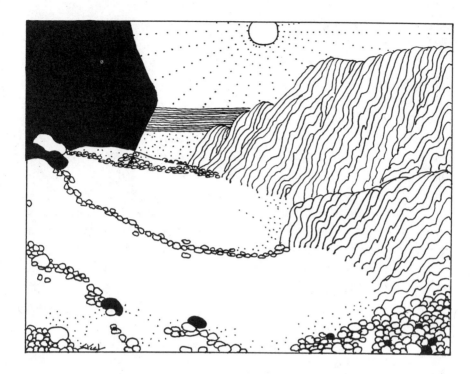

feeling that had overtaken me on the fringes of the sandneck, but the rainproof paper went soft and the questions continued just under the surface of my wet, spattered drawing. How long had the shells lain there like wind-picked skeletons? What were the bones? Why were they fragmented when the snail cases — infinitely more fragile — lay undamaged? What fires had reddened the few round stones? were they campfires, or wildfires? Had Time placed these moments in layers, or had things happened all at once, the snails, the bones, the stones coming together in some cataclysmic happening that left only the wind to blow through them, and no memory at all?

"Mary?" I called. But I realized the others had gone on — the lighthouse, they had said.

I crossed back through the eerie pocket of the dunes, stopping once to retrieve a small white snail shell. I held it in my open hand. It was a perfect intricate whorl of calcium, a whorl of once-living material that had been centrifuged in slow motion not perceptible to the human eye. The operculum was missing. Light flooded the open doorway into this tiniest of worlds, but nothing was being nourished by that light. The life had slipped away; the entry had become an exit.

Wouldn't the hermits have had a time? I thought, as I placed the shell in my pocket the way Demi had done moments ago. When the shell was on the mantel at home, it would remind me that I must come back, to make time for the place of bones and the solving of an unsolved mystery.

I left the sandneck with its questions and went back to the beach to follow the others. They had gone up an old plank road. When I caught up to them, they were standing at the gate to the lighthouse, by a fenced yard that contained dazzling white buildings and a manicured lawn with grass all shorn to a short, even stubble.

"It's three hundred steps down to the sea if you want to go on," Mary said with a sigh. I ran my fingers over the trim white picket fence. Green lawn showed through the slats, neat, tidy.

The fog had cut visibility outside the lighthouse gate to ten feet, and we were surrounded by heavy, leaking clouds. There were 360 fog-drifted steps if we wanted to stare out at an ocean we couldn't see for fog. From Mary's hair poured rivulets of rain as she waited for my answer, and my head, still full of a lingering uneasiness, couldn't leave the Sandneck mystery. "Another time?" I suggested.

"We're going back to camp to light a fire," said Theresa. "And make tea," added Demi. They disappeared back down the plank road. I fell into step behind Mary.

"Tea would be ambrosia right now," she said.

The trails back to camp had turned to muddy freshets. To the left and then the right we passed the Sandneck without speaking. In my pocket my hand closed over a tiny fragile shell, a reminder that here was a haunting tale I had yet to discover.

The weather miraculously cleared as we went on camping on the beach of wolves. But, unable to forget the strange Sandneck, I packed a day bag and went alone.

Climbing up between the rocky dunes once more, I was expecting the sun to make everything different, the Sandneck to be free of the oppression that had come with the rain. But

I was wrong; nothing had changed. The eeriness still haunted the place, and around me the bone fragments, the snail shells, seemed to gleam even more starkly white than they had done before. As I walked into the hollow where the red stones lay I seemed to float rather than walk. My feet were light, weightless. I waited for my head to clear and remembered that food, although it hadn't removed the disorientation, had helped assuage it the last time.

I picked a spot quite close to where we had sat when there had been four of us, and I had just begun eating when I saw the man . . . He had obviously been following me — he couldn't have followed me, though. No, he had come from a different direction, and couldn't have seen me until he had rounded the dune.

"Strange place," he said, as he went to pass in front of the spot where I was sitting.

"Very," I answered. I noticed that he was tall and blond; a stubble of beard blurred his features.

"Did you know about the wars that had happened here?" he asked. "But later it was a farm," he added.

"Wars?" I asked.

"Wars between Indians, the Quatsino and the Nahwitti tribes. They fought over the halibut grounds. Later it became a farm." The man looked off over the dunes to the grass, the old fences, the sand-drowned trees. His eyes seemed to weave them together into a pattern of his own thoughts.

I waited, hoping he would elaborate.

"One day, when the settlers were still farming, some Indians came with sacks. They began gathering up bones; they said it was their ancestors, they were going to take the bones to a new village. They didn't want to leave them here, they said, in this place of sorrow, but to take them to a sacred place. One old Indian had described the battle. All the people were killed, he said; he had been there. He had been a small boy and he had hidden under the body of his mother. That old Indian man had been the only survivor."

"No wonder the place seems strange," I said, realizing finally the cause of my disorientation. I had been sensitive to the uncomfortable past of the sands. "I felt as if something terrible had happened here," I said. "I get strange feelings sometimes. I kept feeling the Sandneck was some sort of terrible place." I shivered in the noonday sun.

"Yes, it is," said the man, as he hitched the pack he carried higher on his shoulder and made a move to trudge on.

"It's great weather for a walk to the lighthouse," I added, thinking he would take the 360 steps in stride; he looked athletic.

"Yes," said the man, "but I've some work to do." He went off, talking over his shoulder. I thought I heard him say harrowing, then thought I hadn't heard clearly. *Harrowing?* Here? It wasn't all that easy to understand the Scandinavian accent. I turned back to the silence of the dunes.

I pulled out the bleached snail shell and walked with it curled in my hand. I tried concentrating on it. The life of its occupant certainly seemed less complicated than mankind's. The thought of a child hiding under his mother's mutilated body sent chills through the hot day. I was on a ground of bloodshed. The bones, I thought . . . Talking to the man had only deepened my disorientation.

I crossed over the neck to the northwest-facing beach and sat down on a sandy shelf, trying to breathe myself free. The sun clapped a warm hand on my back. It was soothing to stroke the sand beside the rare corkwing plants as I sat. The sand of history, I thought. I'm trying to smooth over the sand of history . . .

The bank was warm, and my imagination ironed out the rough bits of a past that was blowing away with time. Then my hand contacted something in the sand. Several small bird bones, delicate and fragile, that lay just under the surface. I placed them in a row; then my hand touched something smooth and pointed. I let the object precede my finger out of the sand into the daylight. It was another bone fragment, this one pointed at both ends, a bone — but — *altered* . . . I put the fragment on my knee and sat looking at it for long moments. A halibut lure!

Everything slipped into place. The Sandneck, although it had known war, had also had been a place of hunter-gatherers. On this battlefield had been fashioned not

just weapons, but implements of peace and work. In my mind Indian people pulling halibut into dugout canoes began to obliterate the bloody scene of the child hiding under his mother's body from the terrors of war. In those moments of sunlight the halibut lure seemed infinitely precious. It held man's better potential.

For a moment, I thought what a conversation piece the old lure would make on my coffee table, but I was prompted another way. It belongs here among the stones and the bones, where it can go on making its statement about human endeavour in a place scoured out by bloodshed. I held it, while something argued it was another souvenir, in the light of day, poised over my day pack; another treasure. Then, with a swift single movement, I slipped it into its rightful place deep in the sands of the mysterious Sandneck.

# 16. Land of Dreams

 IN THE distance the girls were tiny specks at the farthest end of the shore. Between us was the resounding roar of a pounding white surf.

"Damn it!" said Mary. "You'd think they would set up camp at this end of the beach and save us another two-mile hike with the packs. Camping by a river is only inviting bears to pay a visit. What if the one we saw at Fisherman Bay wants a drink or to fish in the creek for supper?"

The tides on the east end of the beach had made a trash dump of logs, a giant's game of pickup sticks. Theresa and Demi's tent stood in the only clear patch of sand. What was left for us was a small patch lower down. The two girls sat on the logs watching Mary and I become ants, rearranging, building, clearing off debris. When Demi got tired she looked at a scrap she had torn from a tide book. "We're going to have a record low tide in the morning," she said. "Why don't we get up early?"

"Why don't we get up and combine suppers?" said Theresa. She inveigled our help to turn over an old crab crate and make a dinner table.

We searched the last of our stores for contributions in the hopes of making our stew a gastronomic delight: rice, noodles, (no miso,) cabbage, onions. Mexican cheese dip would certainly add a flavour.

"At least it's colourful," said the girls.

"What's that?" said sharp-eyed Mary.

"It's not miso," I said. Was she suspicious of what I had put in the stew? Then I saw that she was looking down the beach. Coming directly toward us was something blacker than anything else in the landscape.

"Bear!" we said in unison.

"Noisemakers!" shouted Mary, who had read all the books about bear attacks. "We need noisemakers!" She grabbed the stewpot. Theresa and Demi began to smack stones together. In a phalanx we advanced down the beach, leaving the rest of our food behind us. But our orchestra was like tinkling cymbals against the roar of the surf, and the bear kept coming.

"Doesn't work!" shouted Mary, as she banged the stewpot with its lid, the contents splashing inside. "I'd rather face the sea than get mauled!" she shouted over her shoulder as she headed to the breakers. "I'll give the bear this food."

"But . . . our food! It's all we've got!" I shouted after her, as I grabbed the cache bag and headed for the woods.

The bear was now within one hundred feet of Mary at the

surf line and sniffing ominously in her direction. I searched for a tree with a limb I could reach with the rope, and turned to look back just in time to see the bear and Mary standing face to face, with fifty feet between them. The bear sniffed disdainfully, then, turning on its heels, it sauntered up the beach in the direction of the bush. The two girls had stopped their performance with the rocks. They, too, stood staring.

Mary returned on rubber legs. "We have to build a big fire," she said. "A great big one to keep the animals away!"

We started with twig parings and ended up with whole logs, and still Mary goaded us to greater efforts. The fire grew. "It'll keep the animals away," Mary reiterated, in a frenzy of dragging over whatever she could lift. "And Creosote logs — they'll hate it!"

Environmental consciousness disappeared. We threw logs on until the fire raged. "I know, I know," said Mary. "But I'm not going to spend the night in the bear capital of the world without a good fire."

The bushes trembled and crackled as I combed the driftpile at the top of the beach. The bear was still there waiting on the fringes of our camp. I didn't tell the others.

"We'll need a lamp for tonight," said Mary, when she stopped stoking. "Let's look for a plastic bottle and make a storm lantern."

The beach was littered with trash. We soon had a bleach bottle lamp between our beds as insurance for investigating night noises. Sensing a disrupted slumber, I announced before crawling into my sleeping bag that nothing, absolutely nothing, would induce me to leave my bed during the night. "We're totally vulnerable to bears," said I. "If I'm roused from sleep to worry about that, I'll never sleep at all. There's nothing I can do short of playing dead — which sleep resembles anyway. So I'm going to sleep right through and let the bears rummage around. After all, we've never brought food into the tent; why would they want to come indoors? No snufflings, snortings or rutting-arounds will induce me to stick my head up out of the covers tonight."

Bidding everyone goodnight, and leaving Mary throwing another creosoted log on the fire, I rolled myself up in my

bag with finality for the day; then I closed my eyes, buried my ears, and went to sleep the sleep of the dead.

Sometime during the night through the thick pad of down over my ears I heard something rustling. I opened one eye. Mary was struggling into her coat. She went sliding out into a fresh fall of rain.

Keeping my promise of not moving until the morning, I remained still, feigning sleep, but I could feel the wind blowing into the open doorway of the tent, the patter of rain on my head. "I wish you'd shut the damn flap instead of letting the dampness in," I called after her, but I could hear her stoking the fire, logs crackling outside. I shrank away from the mist of rain in the open doorway. I snugged blankets more tightly over my ears, around my face. Fine way to keep things dry, I thought.

"Are you awake?" Mary called through the thin nylon wall. She must have been standing right outside, not a foot from my ear.

"M-m-m-m," I mumphed from the depths of my imagined protection.

There was alarm in her voice. "Maybe you should know that the last wave came up to within five feet of the fire."

Silence.

"The surf's going to swamp the tent any minute."

Silence.

"Maybe you should get up and take a look at this."

Then I was wide awake and still refusing to move.

"What about staying here out of the rain for another half hour?" I suggested to the heavy human silence that waited outside. "If the surf hits the fire we'll hear it sizzle. We can move the tent then — but to who knows where?" I muttered as I thought of the piles of logs covering the sand. Still, I readied myself for a grand exodus out of my bag and into my clothes. Thoughts of bear attacks faded into all-engulfing tides. Wouldn't the beach let us have any peace?

Reluctantly Mary climbed in, and we sat on our beds. Above the angry crackling of the fire was the steady drumming of rain on the tent roof and the roar of the waves running up the beach, each one coming nearer. Our ears waited for that final hiss between the elements, water drowning fire — five minutes — ten minutes. Time heightened the intensity of waiting. We perched on our beds, fight-or-flight in our minds.

"The sea on one side of us, bears on the other, a deluge above, and sticks and stones below." Mary wasn't cheering me up, either. "I'm going out to have another look," she added.

Within minutes she was back, her face awash with relief. "I think the worst is over; the tide has changed. And wouldn't you know, the girls didn't even stir? We could drown and they wouldn't notice till morning."

We threw off our jackets, and settled down once more to drift away on tides of sleep.

After that there were more bear sounds, but not even Mary stirred. And then it was almost dawn and Theresa and Demi stood outside our door flap. Time to hit the beach, they said, if we wanted to explore while the tide was at its lowest. They did not wait for us to respond.

Mary and I struggled from our beds. Did we really want to do this? But I reached for my journal and pen; a tide like this mustn't go unrecorded. The chance of being on this beach again during minus tides was negligible. Fumbling in

the predawn darkness, I crawled over and poked my head out of the tent door. In the half-light all I could see was a wall of mist and desolation . . . and the two girls, yellow-slickered dots fading into dark along the beach. Never in my own life before or since have I seen such a dark, remote and abysmal scene.

I found myself wondering how many mornings of grey, drizzling emptiness had greeted Nels Nelsen when he spent his winter alone in this forbidding place, cut off from the world. How did he and Hansen, or any of the settlers, last for thirty-five years on the shores of Cape Scott, this land of their dreams?

A crew member on Captain Cook's ship, *Resolution*, when he had seen the coastline of Vancouver Island had remarked, " A more dreary prospect I never yet came the way of . . . "

I shuddered in the damp dawn air and crawled back into my cold sleeping bag to wait for a little more of the day to make itself visible.

# 17.  Keeshan

"TAKE IT easy going over," Mary called out, as I disappeared below the jutting bow of Raven Moon into a vertical tangle of undergrowth. My kayak pivoted on a fulcrum of bush, eager to slide down the embankment into Bamfield Inlet. With one hand around an alder sapling, I grasped her bow and held her.

*Raven Moon* jerked at the end of the rope. This was not the time to let thoughts wander.

"Are you okay?" came Mary's voice. "Can I let go?"

Before I could answer, she released the bow rope and *Raven Moon* careened down the bank. I, too, lost my hold and went sliding down to crash beside her. I scrambled up to my feet, brushed away a litter of earth crumbs and then realized that my performance had not gone unnoticed. A group of fishermen loading a nearby gillnetter had stopped what they were doing. They stood staring. I heard laughter, but there was no time to warn Mary.

"Stephanie? Are you still there?" she called out. Then, without waiting for an answer, her kayak hurtled down the slope.

"Here it comes!" The boat flew out over the last eight feet of undercut, landed on the beach, bounced three times and slid across the mud and barnacles to arrive beside *Raven*

*Moon* with a thump. Mary followed her boat, arriving beside me in a shower of debris.

"A plastic boat is great," she said, dusting herself off. "No worries." She gave a scornful look in *Raven Moon*'s direction and began poking her supplies ahead of her footrest with her paddle.

"Great for pushing down banks," I muttered under my breath, "but a Tupperware boat is no queen of the high seas."

We decked in, climbed aboard and with eyes straight ahead, parted the waters past the heron-eyed fishermen.

Ahead of us lay the village of Bamfield across the bridgeless channel, with all its charm laid out and hooked together by boardwalks. In a moment of appreciation we shipped paddles and drifted past the sleepy village. The early morning was turning the seaweed gold.

We were off again, a new year and a new adventure. And even though I knew *Raven Moon* should be sailing the Seven Seas, not sailing over a tangled bank and puddling up a muddy inlet, I looked forward to reaching the coast by kayak and foot. Our paddles shattered the stillness of the quiet waters that lay ahead.

On our trek to Cape Scott the previous year, I had told Mary of my interest in seeking even older remnants of B.C. life than those left by the Danish settlers. What about the remains of the original inhabitants, I had said. The halibut hunters, the whale people?

We searched old records in the Provincial Archives. When we discovered a newspaper article on a coastal village called Keeshan and known as Execution Rock we decided to make the search for it our next summer project.

We followed the sun into the inlet as it pierced the tops of the cedars that fringed the shore. The cedars didn't rot when they died, they poked bare tridents skyward. "They've formed their own mortuary columns," said Mary.

"Eagles' roosts," said I. It was an eerie landscape. "Lucky the eagles aren't vultures."

We soon became trapped in the sluggish quagmire of a minus tide. I had to start using my paddle as a pry. "Talk about croutons sliding around in a great soup bowl of mud," I said, trying to make light of our troubles.

"Will we make it to shore?" asked Mary, as her boat squeaked ominously on the mud below. "Maybe the wharf?" She pointed with a weed-thickened paddle to a jetty that led to the house where we planned to ask permission to cross the Indian reserve. "Or shall we just get out into this and disappear? Our families would never understand what had happened," she added, as she used her hands to push herself and her kayak over the muck towards the nearest sedgey bank. I put a hand down to the gelatinous bottom and the mud rose in clouds. I scrunched up my behind as if I could lift it out of the way as I turtled myself ashore.

By the time we had scrambled out, shoved our kayaks out of sight under low-hanging evergreens and reached the house, our boots resembled the hooves of Clydesdales. I stood behind Mary and saw that the Native woman's eyes never left our feet as she pointed to a variegated ribbon of mudholes, bear pats and wild tracks.

"The bear tracks are huge," said Mary, as we set out.

"Maybe their feet were caked with mud, too," I offered.

"Don't kid yourself; bears are not puppies."

She said it again when we came to the bearhole that

local residents had told us was the start of the trail that led to Execution Rock. Mary went first, disappearing downwards into the darkness of the unknown. I followed. Just another tumble down another embankment.

We headed along the beach, wondering, wondering — had we got the right bearhole? Were we to turn right or left? Neither of us knew.

"What a fortress!" said Mary, mouth open at the sight of the rock bluff. "That's it — no mistaking it!"

Execution Rock cut a facetted wedge out of the blue sky. At the far end was a rock turret with bonsai trees.

Somewhere from the depths of the great rock that sat by itself a sea chasm moaned tragically. "Listen," I said. "It's telling the tale of the children of Keeshan."

We put down our day packs at the top of the shelving beach. The trail zigzagged up a smooth grass bank, rising steeply. I removed my sketchbook and carried it one-handed.

"Look out!" shouted Mary, pointing at a large patch of salal dead ahead. The wide leaves and tangled stems hid thin air underneath. I was poised over emptiness, my feet ready to step onto a few thin stalks of plant. I looked through at the little sea patches between the leaves and gasped at how high we had climbed. "Without warning!" I breathed.

"They used to push young men over that to see if they would survive," said Mary. "It was like an initiation into manhood. The article said so."

"Don't believe everything you read," said I, when I got my breath back. "No one would survive a fall from here."

We went higher, to the summit, into a tangle of trees and dark earth and crumbled shale. "You might be right about the truth and newspaper articles," said Mary. "There's certainly no room on the top for five longhouses."

"Nothing to show," said I. But Mary began poking at the remnants of a low wall along the cliff edge.

"This could have been manmade," she said at last. "Remember, the articles said the villagers built a wall to stop children from falling over the edge."

"I don't see the shaft where the children hid. I don't see signs of longhouses, either."

"Don't you remember, they filled it in with whalebones?" I watched Mary wander off, talking to herself, along the side of the abutment.

I walked to the edge of the rock, and stood looking out over the water. What had it been like, I wondered, when the sentries of Keeshan had watched for the return of the Clallums? If I were one of the Ohiaht, would I ever have stopped worrying that the enemy might come back?

I sat down on the old cracked rock, dizzy with the height of looking at the ocean below. For a while I concentrated on a small poque plant that grew near the edge. Dependant on salal bush for food, poque was a rare thing to see, sticking up out of the ground like a bright yellow upraised spruce cone. The Pokmis — spirit of the drowned! The Indians used to eat it — more proof. Then something tripped the legend out of my memory, out of my thinking and from the bush, and the trees, and the poque, in the village of Keeshan that had come to be known as

Execution Rock. I saw the impression of a longhouse amongst the trees that grew on the bluff. It was a chief's longhouse, a place of ceremonies; and beside me, half hidden in the loose crumbling rock, was a hidden crack. It widened into a secret cavern as it ran down through the rocks to the beach below. I looked into the crack. It went deep and dark with years, and I drifted down through them as my mind travelled inward, seeking.

It had started with a bloody skirmish over fishing rights. As was the custom of coastal tribes in B.C., the conquering Ohiahts of Keeshan had impaled the heads of their victims of the Clallum tribe on stakes around the shore in a gruesome display of strength.

Afterward, the village of Keeshan feared a reprisal. They waited months for the return of the Clallum people for a war of vengeance. But time stretched out, and not once did the Clallums return. The village got tired of watching. The people even forgot the psychic warning of a dying shaman who had advised the Ohiahts of the village of Keeshan to beware of coming dark moons, for enemies were near. Life simply picked up its stitches and went on.

The chiefs of Keeshan became preoccupied with holding The Tlokwana, the wolf festival, in which elected people of the village dressed in costumes, grey blankets pulled down over their foreheads to represent wolves' muzzles. These wolves would hide in the forest. They would make repeated mock attacks on the village to seize young chosen initiates and drag them away into the woods. Then mock armed parties would go looking through the village and into the woods, searching for the wolves. Supernatural sound effects, using whistles, bullroarers and drums made out of hollow logs, would heighten the disruption of normal village life. Fearful anticipation would be followed by panic and flight. Pandemonium would take over the village, driving it to fever pitch. After four days the children would be returned and there would be a great celebration with processions and the singing of spirit songs, dancing and merrymaking. The balsam bough costumes that the children had worn would be burned in a ceremonial fire, while the drums would drive the wolves back into the forest.

Four days of the festival had gone by and the drumming was ear splitting. The wolves had been called repeatedly. The armed parties had returned empty-handed. Then suddenly, the children had been seen wandering along the beach. Triumphantly they were brought back to the village to sing their spirit songs and burn their costumes.

In the excitement of The Tlokwana, any thought of posting sentries vanished in the smoke of the ceremonial fire. Then darkness came without moonlight. On the water, five canoes bearing soot-darkened warriors pulled up on the beach.

The muffled footsteps and the sound of wood on sand were swallowed up in the songs and the drumming and the wild firelight celebrations on the rock above. The burning of the balsam branch clothing sent showers of sparks into the air. The Clallums waited motionless in the darkness while their emissary went up the trail carrying a firebrand. If all the Ohiahts were inside the longhouse at the fire pit, the spy was to cast the glowing torch over the edge of the cliff to the beach below.

The signal came, a fiery ember plunging seaward, sparks scattering from it as it flew. It singed, steaming into the water and, with a hiss, died back into night.

In unison the Clallums rose. One by one they moved across the beach, clutching their slave killers. They climbed the thin, winding trail past the bank where the salal hid the sheer cliff, past the logs that had been piled in readiness to roll down on intruders.

The noise of the celebrations mingled in the lighted air with the sparks from the fire pit as more of the balsam bough costumes were consigned, spitting and crackling, to the fire.

With a wild yell that was far more bloodcurdling than any of the sounds of The Tlokwana, the Clallums attacked.

The Keeshans were unarmed, and the killing was easy. The battle was over in a matter of minutes. There would have been no survivors if it hadn't been for the hidden shaft that led to the beach below. Shivering from the shock and the cold, four children cowered. All night long they clung to the wet rocks, knowing that to reveal themselves was to die. Around them everything became deathly still.

When at last a shaft of soft light flickered among the

evergreens and came alive with the calling of the ravens outside, the terrified children knew that it was daytime — and that if they continued clinging to their perch in the shaft they would soon perish from the cold. Blinking away the fierce light, they ventured out.

Before them lay the horror of the ransacked village. Headless bodies of their families were strewn on blood-spattered ground, some on the path, others on the rocks below. Smashed and destroyed remnants of their home and belongings lay scattered on the beach.

With strong presence of mind, the children searched the rubble until they found an old canoe half rotting in the deep bush above the sea. Between the four of them they dragged the boat over the layers of kelp. The survivors left Keeshan without looking back. It would be years before they returned to rebuild their lost village.

"I think I've found something," called Mary from the beach far below. I was forced out of the rock crack into the present day. The legend vanished.

"Do you think this is the spot where the wooden welcome figures stood, the ones that now stand at the entrance to Thunderbird Park in Victoria? It seems the perfect place for the figures of a man and woman fifteen feet tall," she said. "And this lone post could easily have been part of a longhouse." She began pushing deeper into the bush. "Look!" she said more emphatically, as she parted the wall of salmon-berry plants and disappeared inside. "Longhouses!"

Five great posts among the trees jumped into recognition. Then more — then more! As our eyes grew accustomed to the gloom inside the woods, great crossbeams formed the pattern of longhouses. Ferns and massive growing cedars as big in girth as the roof poles themselves jutted skyward from the top surfaces. Around five great rectangles that had once been longhouses, moss had reclaimed Keeshan. Her artifacts were hidden from view. "The coastal wilderness just takes it back," I said, as I swept an arm over the forest for emphasis. The moss was fragile, and the patch where I touched it came off in my hand. Under it lay a mound of whalebones.

I sat down with my sketchbook in the heart of something historic. I became engrossed in the drawing of it.

When we left the site of Keeshan to return to our kayaks, I was vaguely dissatisfied. I had not been able to catch the size of the great forest dwellings any more than the old faded newspaper photograph we had pored over in the archives had caught the size of the rock fortress. It had not trapped any feeling of the struggles to live and survive on this rugged coast. Perhaps the mound of whalebones told it best, or the loose crumbling rock of the bluff, or the forest growth that was inexorably wiping away the adze-marked wood and the last human touch of the Coast whaling village that once was Keeshan.

"You know," I said to Mary as we left to recover our kayaks and paddle against the flooding tide down Bamfield Inlet, "I wish I could just draw the feeling of the place, just freeze Keeshan in time, before it's gone forever."

"You have to just let it go," said Mary, in a moment of wisdom. "That's its charm. You can't stop the forest from reclaiming it. There are other villages, but we might have to go further to find them — Nootka Island, why don't we try that?"

"Why Nootka Island?" I asked.

"That's where the white people made such an impact with the Native people. The Nootka Convention and all that. Have you heard of John Jewitt, who was the captive of Maquinna and the Moachaht people for two years? Maybe we'd find something there, more longhouses. I can't get over looking at those huge buildings made with only manpower and stone tools. You could paint those. Emily Carr did and look how famous she got . . . . "

I did not hold forth with my views on fame. I realized we had left Keeshan in the quiet of its past. We were touching momentarily on the present, and now were going off with the future. Eagles would go back to their roosts in the cedar trees, and darkness would take Keeshan. There was a story there that would never make it into the history books. As we turned the first point and Keeshan faded from view, I glanced back and saw the sunlight gilding the legend for only a moment's passing.

# 18.    Three Generations of Abandonment

WE HAD made it to the Queen Charlottes. After our explorations at Nootka Island and the rock at Keeshan, we had spread ever further to seek remnants of old B.C. Now we were ready for a hike along the east coast of Graham Island, to explore the beach and look for the sites of old villages. In the evening of our first day we abandoned the domestic scene of setting up camp and set off down the east side of the Tlell River for a walk.

I stood drawing the structure of an abandoned pioneer home of logs and puddled clay and its attendant outhouse that ballooned with honeysuckle vine. Heady scent pervaded the evening air, the human scent long dissipated by ten thousand winds. Behind the buildings I found an old truck marked Wells Fargo, sunk to its knees in the long grass. Beside it an open well made of drainage culvert invited the careless to drop in. Looking down into the hole, I was relieved to see no sign of skeletons.

Peering through a window into the main house, I saw an empty room set up with dining table and chairs. The space looked hauntingly cut off by the panes of glass, the dim light and a locked door. My mind saw the lace, the silverware of past times; but there were no people.

The skeleton of an umbrella functioning as a radio aerial

on the peak of the roof lent an increasing note of the bizarre. A six-paned window, tucked away at the end of the building, shed dim light on a workshop. Three old fishing plugs hooked by invisible filament to the wooden frame caught my attention. Wooden fish swam endlessly upward in a dusty wood-framed aquarium — a surrealistic painting, images frozen in time.

The place exuded abandonment; how could I put the finger of reason solidly on my thoughts in a place like this?

Mary startled me. She had found an old 1960s bus deep in the woods, some nomad's home that had come to a sad sag in the depths of the bush.

"Where do people go?" she asked. Something like a shadow ran through her eyes. That same feeling . . .

I finished sketching and we headed off along the banks of the river toward the sea.

"There's another empty place," said Mary, stopping up short.

"Hardly empty. It's full of no-seeums!" said I, as we stopped to zip up our jackets and tighten our drawstring hoods. The bugs headed out of open doors and windows like a black cloud. With slotted eyes I watched Mary disappear

inside the building. The uninvited guest, I thought — just walking in . . .

"Look, it's clean, not even vandalized." Her face was framed by a wind-tattered plastic tarpaulin in a glassless window. I was seeing another painting. Windows trapped scenes. Windows recalled past occupants.

"Someone has lavished love and care on this residence; I wonder where they went," Mary said, as her hand strayed over the built-in furniture once highly polished. Then we stood outdoors, remarking that the landscape was part of the package of who lived here.

"For two cents I'd move in — lock, stock and barrel." Mary stood watching the slow river outside. It played with strands of drifting seaweed come inland from the sea. "No more highways, no more nine-to-five, endless peace and quiet . . . it seems perfect."

"Endless no-seeums," I replied, and wiped my face clear one more time of a beard of tiny black corpses. "The flies seem to have the tenacity humans lack. They stay on to inherit what their ancestors leave. Humans don't seem to do that anymore."

We left the house to the passing winds of Tlell and went in search of old fishing wickiups rumoured to be on the river mouth.

We followed a line of old grape fencing into the dunes. On the drifted sand were notched posts. We had found what we were looking for, the oldest of the old. The wood was grooved deep; all the soft parts had been blown away to passing seasons, everything on the beach scoured clean. The wood was old — old — older than anything.

"Not much left," I muttered. "Maybe one hundred years from now that cedar home will also be all blasted out like this. Why do people leave?"

Our questions left us wondering about life, about hardship. I was beset with the surrealist dream once more. A picture of my home in Deep Cove flashed by. It was derelict; the wind blew through its slats. All at once I knew wind was not the enemy, bulldozers were not the enemy. The enemy was time itself. It showed in the empty shelters of other human beings.

"You know, I sometimes feel I'm abandoning my real life," I said suddenly. "My home in Deep Cove and what my existence really is — taking on the life I conceive of being free and footloose. It's living a lie, really. But if you do pursue that life, then it becomes real and the other drops by the wayside."

"That's too deep," said Mary. "Let's go back to camp and make tea."

We had not gone far on our way back when our movement was interrupted by black dots drifting in the river. We stopped. Was it otters? Seals? No. Deer were crossing the slow-moving water. Passing on the edge of darkness, silent shadows swam, leaving streaks of light in their wake. Effortlessly they gained the far bank, danced up on stick-thin legs full of grace, then crossed where the sun still slanted golden light up the banks onto Tlell sands. They went foraging up into the grasses of the dunes and, ghostlike, disappeared.

"They've been crossing in that spot for thousands of years, since time immemorial," I whispered. "For them there's no abandonment."

I looked over at Mary. She seemed lost in a tragedy of her own.

We headed to our camp with no more conversation. Our small tent city was calling us back to a place of life, to sleep, a place to eat, warmth of a down bag, warmth of a cooking fire, good company. Silently we performed a tiny ritual that was merely a pinprick in space and time. We heated up tea on the gas stove and turned in to a night of stars.

# 19.  Winds of Cape Ball

THE BREAKERS crashed early and came in thundering. Above the surf the drift was piled high along the berm. Basted by the sun, the rain and the wind, old logs had lain undisturbed above the tides for years. Among them sand had been ground fine and soft, piled deep. We were travelling light. "Leave all but the barest essentials because of the soft sand," Mary had said.

I packed my sleeping bag, granola and a can of sardines. We would share Mary's tent.

But then, when I wanted to sketch the old beach wreck, I realized I had forgotten my art supplies.

"How could I leave everything that's important to me behind — and all just for travelling light? I'd sooner have carried fifty pounds and come with what I needed." I stomped a circle of anger into the sand. "This trip is the epitome of parsimony."

"Sleeping bags, plastic wrap and half a tent each." Mary lifted her pack with one hand and smiled a smile I couldn't share. "I'm sick of being burdened down with a whole lot of camping gear. This way we'll get to Cape Ball in half the time."

We walked as if each of us were alone on the beach. Without book or pen I was in a changing landscape unprepared.

We set up Mary's tent that night by the Mayer River, and

sat down beside the stream where the water pooled at the top of the beach. "I guess you're missing your things," said Mary.

"How can I just let this scene go by unrecorded?" I said.

We sat not speaking, while small fish dotted the surface of the pond with Zen moments. I paid no heed. Sheltering us from ocean breezes, unstable dunes teetered on the edge of collapse into the small brown stream at their base. They whispered of peace descending with the quiet trickle of sand down a sloping surface, but I couldn't feel it.

Mary reminded me that we had come to look for K'ahlenskun. I squinted into the afternoon light. What purpose to look when I had no materials for recording what I saw? "Perhaps K'ahlenskun is totally buried," I said, trying to make light of a dark mood. "Perhaps in a hundred years people will come looking for your tent, Mary, when it's buried by an unexpected dune, or a sandstorm."

"Go on," said Mary.

"They'll call it a wickiup, too, like the fish shelter at Tlell River. I bet that's a name the West Coast people never even heard of."

"It's no different than calling the natives Indians," said Mary. She wandered off between the dunes. Moments later she was back. "I think I've found something — and perhaps it's K'ahlenskun."

The lodge remains were perched in a hollow tucked between a group of dying trees. It was barely more than a scoop in the sand and two timbers showing adzework, the human touch, underneath the sandblast.

"How did you find it?" I asked.

"People come and go, don't they?" she said. "There's almost nothing left."

We stood looking over the drift of sand to the lee of the dunes. For a moment I saw it sifting grain by grain out to shore and the sea, in a long flowing movement. Like sand in an egg timer, I thought. In such a harsh place wind and tide had scoured out the soft, the movable. What to the sea's expanse was a small lodge and a family of people? A strange, inhospitable place, this British Columbia, I thought; yet on

the surface it looked enticing, and the longhouse people had remained at least for a time.

By evening, the dark mood had left me with many loose ends. How dependant I had become on pens and paper and a book to read. I waded across the stream's emptying shallows, my feet sinking among shells, crackling them underfoot. I wanted to be drawing. What was life without it? I tried to distract myself by beachcombing instead, but human flotsam and jetsam was missing. A knotted piece of driftwood transposed itself to the mantel in my remembered home far away, but the gnarled piece was too heavy; I'd not be willing to carry it back to Deep Cove calling it treasure. I poked it up among the logs. My empty arms carried only the memory of how easy and plentiful treasure was any other time.

In this place the current scoured almost daily up to the edge of the cliffs, depositing wood and removing it in an endless game. I watched the evening light dance across the sand banks, teasing me with sketches. Paintings formed in my mind and sifted away like the dune sands around our camp. I found no satisfaction. I'm addicted to art, I realized. I've come this far in my life and now I can't be happy without my things. I lay in my bed that night trying not to disturb Mary, a cocoon-like lump in exactly half of her tent. I realized I had only just managed the one day without my art supplies.

Grey skies loomed over the morning; a twenty-eight-day record of drought was on perilous ground.

"It's nothing more than morning mist," said Mary, as we battened the door of the tent with the backpacks inside. We would not take them on our trek to Cape Ball.

As we started out along the base of the sand banks, we talked of the cliffs we had seen from the deck of the *Queen of Prince Rupert* when we had crossed Hecate Strait toward Graham Island. The sun had turned them to a gleaming line of light on the horizon, shining against the pile skirt of a restless sea.

"Are we going to hike that?" we both had said.

Today the rain pitted them; mist withdrew in threads along the top of the ridge, leaving scattered patterns of light against the tall, sandy banks. Remembering a dream I had had during the night, in which I was carrying an empty beggar's bowl across a desert, I decided to work on my memory rather than go empty-handed. I decided to make a mental list, to catalogue the scenes in my mind that I would later want to paint. I soon had a strip — like movie film going around in my head. Then Mary shouted, "Look — agates!" Along the beach the gems glittered, distracting the light. Begging to be picked up, they punctured my strip of scenes.

"We should save agate-gathering for the beach at Tow Hill," said Mary. "We won't need to backpack them out to the car there."

In a display of nonchalance, I tossed a handful aside. My other scenes were gone, but I had this one. I'll call it "Sparkling Beach," I thought to myself, but no sooner thought, the scene glittered with fractured light and danced away from my eyes.

We travelled beside low sand banks. Tussock grass clasped fronds and roots tenaciously over the tops to hold things in place. At eye level glimpses of small green meadows above the beach beckoned me to the unknown. I left Mary walking the tideline and climbed to a small sand field that ran parallel to the sea. Beside it was an umber dark bog hemmed by young evergreens six to ten feet in height. The saplings had been nibbled into shrubs by foraging deer. They had pruned the spruce trees to dense sharp cones. Their needles scratched my legs. Around me pungent bear dung lay in clumps of serious warning. Black shadows inside the wood glowered. Peeking over the bank, I saw Mary, a dot in the distance, hopelessly far away.

I began to sing loudly enough to alert any bears of my presence. When I narrowly missed stepping into a steaming bear pat, my voice went up an octave. In the dark of the bush a great rustling of branches told me something was trying to escape my attempt at song. As I moved back in the direction of the beach, I saw the ramshackle lean-to. Hiding against the wall of forest with only a peephole of view out onto the sea, with boards that had been cleaned by the elements and the densest part of the woodgrain standing out in bas-relief, it clung like a crone, old, dried out, low to the earth. It hugged the dense shrubbery and hid from something unimaginable.

I couldn't approach — perhaps someone . . . but only the sighing wind on dry sand sent a whisper when I breathed a tentative hello to the ghost occupant.

What a great subject for sketching, said the dreamer in me, as I sank down onto the tussock grass beside it, bears forgotten. For long moments my eyes traced around the scene, embracing it, but a mental photograph, I realized, wouldn't be enough. It just wouldn't last. My hands scrabbled around me until they connected with a twig; I began to use it to scratch on a patch of bare sand, but the sand was soft; it fell back into its own hole, swallowing my drawing as rapidly as I created it. My pulse began to pound at double time. Catch it, the artist said. I scratched harder, deeper, until suddenly, wraithlike, my thoughts drifted up on wind spirals and turned to look down on me.

With a shudder I collapsed to the present. What had I been looking at? In that moment — a crazy woman, living wild in the sands, spending herself on foolish scratchings with frail thin sticks for drawing and living under old thin boards, her skin as dry and sandblasted as they. The bears would not be attracted to flesh so old and withered, and the art would sift away grain by grain on stiff winds, the rain would pock the lot.

*Masterpieces*. The old woman was still there. Rain and wind just make their own . . .

Why do you do it? What is it you want? came a question on the wind. Is it fame? No. Do you want your work to hang in Important Galleries? In museums — to last? Yes. But there was no posterity in it. People didn't see it, people were manipulated into extremes. Yes, I laughed, they can truck my sand work in — given the new technology and the direction of modern art. And guards to watch that my sand art doesn't deteriorate.

Immortality? Yes — for the art, I explained. That's why I can't make cakes and candles and works in sand; they disappear too fast. Art lasts for ever and ever . . . well — for quite awhile . . . The old woman cackled. She hadn't lost her sense of humour.

Being an artist doesn't matter at all, said the winds of Cape Ball.

But the art does, I argued . . . This place does . . .

Being an artist doesn't matter at all, said the winds of Cape Ball.

I abandoned the place and ran after the dot near the horizon. Spare me from going crazy, my feet seemed to say as they scattered flakes of sand behind me.

When I caught up to Mary, she was sitting beside a meandering stream. She, too, held a twig and was scratching in the sand. Dare I tell her of the crazy woman? She looked puzzled. Why had I come bursting into her reverie all a-clatter?

"I've found the old wagon road to the Giegerich farm," she said instead.

I landed in solid reality.

At K'ahlenskun, legend tells, a prospector once found gold flecks in the running water of the stream. He fetched supplies and set up to live there and mine the creek. He thought of getting rich, but it took longer than he thought, and the winds of Cape Ball did strange things to him. His mind drifted off into the endless, lonely howling of the sands. The shadow of the wraith-like artist spun like a dervish through my consciousness while Mary told the story. The poor prospector eventually had to be led away to what was considered a safer place for him.

I said no word about the crazy woman.

"Did you know there's a rumour that artifacts can be found anywhere from Mayer Creek to the old wreck? That the dunes were solid clamshell from middens at one time? It's all buried, but if one can find a needle in a haystack, perhaps one can try one's luck looking for an artifact in a sand dune."

"I'd sooner go and look in my packsack for something to eat," said Mary. "I'm starved."

I thought of sardines, the last of my food.

"Sardines are dangerous," said Mary.

"What?" said I, all innocence.

"Sardines — because bears can smell them from miles away, even a tin that's been disposed of in a campfire, even if it's buried."

"I'll eat fast, and throw the can into the ocean. It can become a hideout for small fish. Not exactly recycling — but it will have a use there."

"You'll smell good."

Was she thinking of bears, I wondered, or of a night confined with me in her tent?

We both looked at the small tin of food I produced. Our stomachs growled in harmony. Food. Making a ceremony of it, I opened the tin. Mary fetched the last of her crackers, unwrapped them carefully to keep out sand and placed them in a pattern over the plastic wrap. We set the nearest log for a banquet for two. But it was not a dinner for two, for as soon as we were sitting down to our repast a pair of tiny mice, known by oldtimers to be a great rarity on the beaches of Tlell, joined the party. They leapt up on the log, hunger overcoming all inhibitions.

I watched the ravenous pair with their nose hairs twitching. I was suddenly unable to take a bite. "You know, I feel more like walking than eating," I confessed as I stood up. "If you don't want the sardines we could donate them to the mice. I'm just going across the creek — not far."

"What on earth would mice find to eat in a place like this?" said Mary. "It kind of takes away the appetite, doesn't it? I think I'll turn in." Mary took the last of the sardines. As I threw the empty can into the sea, I saw her buttering the last two of her crackers with the fish. She placed them on the log, then she walked to her tent, unzipped the door without looking back and climbed inside.

I began to walk along under the cliffs. I was hungry, but something much deeper than crackers and sardines was needed; food wouldn't do.

I came to the twisted piece of driftwood that I had tucked up among the logs the night before. I realized I had an empty pack for the walk back, no food, no sketchbook. I could take the wood. I have nothing but memories, I thought, and there is room for the driftwood. Would I want to recall memories of paucity and hardship? They would now haunt any trinket I was to bring back. I walked away empty-handed.

I sat on a log and stared up at the wall of cliff above me, at the long expanse of beach running off as far as eye could see, and the long, long roll of breakers lining the beach edge with white. The strip of mental photographs didn't encompass enough, could barely even be recalled. I couldn't help eating, sleeping and breathing art. Everything I did went in its direction, and yet because my thoughts flew around unanchored, unfocused, I had forgotten almost all I had hoped I would remember of the scenes that had come my way. I'm like a fish out of water, I realized, as I stared at the cliff through a blur of manufactured mist.

Impermanence, I thought. That was why the abandoned

buildings had bothered me so much. They stood for the passing of mankind. All his struggles are in vain, I thought.

My eyes followed the striations up the cliff face while the lingering day's light moved across the layers of different-coloured sand that had been compacted and driven into folds by some long past shift and buckle of the Earth's movement. I searched up and up. If I could only see through the layers just one sign of anything indicating human life has a reason, I thought, nothing would be in vain.

I sat for an eon waiting, until my eyes burned dry. The sun was disappearing. I was totally empty, when suddenly a flash just before dark lit up the landscape in clear relief. A golden shaft of light struck the rock and the artist in me was jolted awake! Straining in that moment, in that split second of being, I burst into seeing with fresh eyes. Tiny dots above me, so minute they barely showed, but I had seen them, tiny archetypal creatures, just like the stone loon. With the full thrust of my being I began a journey outward, looking and looking, reaching to strike the mark, some mark somewhere — the mark that belonged to Mankind . . . My mind, haunted by a few meagre years of training, saw suddenly without any training at all.

Quickly I sorted the colours I wanted, removed the lids on the burnt sienna, the burnt umber, the crimson of my mind. I squeezed colour onto an imagined palette, mixed it with care, and just enough. Pausing with the dream brush, I dipped it in one swift familiar movement and began to paint.

I was not trying to interpret the sand of the conglomerate, compressed, about to become stone in its own right on the lowest layers of cliff. What I was painting in my mind was the giant fold and press of the Earth, as if it were dust settling and steam rising. I was attempting to trap a millennia's silent movement of earth into a moment of time that only existed on the imagined paper of my mind, but for an instant there, it lived . . . my brush created the human layer, only a moment of it, near the tip, like a fine dusting of human artifact to claim mankind's right to be heard.

I had created a masterpiece . . . and the Art had come back in the landscape and on the winds of Cape Ball.

# 20.　Plastic

WE FILLED our pockets with agates at Yakan Point. Perhaps in reaction to the parsimony of Cape Ball, we began to fill plastic bags when our pockets overflowed.

When we returned to our camp, we were shocked at the scene we found. Not a single campsite was left at Agate Beach. Our tents had been surrounded by camper trucks, vans and trailers. They had come directly from the Prince Rupert ferry. I remembered my preference for camping nowhere near public campsites.

I dropped my bag of treasures, emptied my pockets, and made the excuse that I was tired. "I'm just not fond of group camps," I said, as I crept inside my tent and closed its walls around me and wished I had the quiet of the dune shelter at Mayer Creek. However, I soon was sleeping the sleep of the fresh-air intoxicated. I awakened in the morning to find a long shadow up my tent wall. Someone was standing outside. A voice suddenly came through the thin cotton walls. I untied the door, lifted the flaps until a bright triangle of sunlight flooded down. There was a woman. Behind her was Mary with her head poking from her tent.

"I'm sorry we were so boisterous last night," said the stranger. "I wondered if a piece of fresh salmon would be a

good peace offering? We ran into friends that we hadn't seen in years," she explained. "And we certainly didn't mean to get so noisy!"

Mary's face had a puzzled look. With a glance at me, I read her thoughts. We scrambled from our tents, accepted the pieces of appeasement with faces like the cat who stole the whipped cream and went to light a cooking fire in our camp grate. Soon all that was left was a few bones and some skin.

"I'll jettison the leftovers into the sea," I said, "just like the legend," and walked down the beach. Mary followed.

"What legend?"

"The one about the Salmon Spirit. About the woman who gave her son a piece of two-year-old dried fish to eat. It was tasteless and tough so the boy stole down to the water and threw it as far out as he could. Suddenly a great fish appeared from the scattered rings made by the skin and bones of the wizened chunk of old fish. It was the strangest, the largest fish the boy had ever seen. He turned to run for his life. But the fish called out, 'Don't run! I am the Spirit of the Salmon People. Thanks to you, I can now resume my proper form and swim free again. When our remains are returned to the ocean, we can, come back. Go and tell the people of your village this is the reason there is such a dearth of fish.'

"So the boy ran back to the village and since that day all Indian people return fish remains to the sea so that the salmon will be abundant."

Eagles circled above the high wall of dark green trees that bordered the steep, driftwood-covered berm. Like them, we had flown the coop and left the busy campsite behind Tow Hill. We walked out onto North Beach, beyond the edge of the sand-drowned trees to the last traces of green. When we stood before skeleton trunks half buried, I stopped walking. My feet throbbed from the long hike. I looked around me for a comfortable perch and collapsed onto a dune at the outer leafless fringe. Ahead lay bare sand and the long hook called Rose Spit. Behind us North Beach ran back to the distant bluff called Tow Hill; though five hundred feet high, the rock had become a walnut in the distance. I looked to the spit and shielded my eyes from the glare.

"That's supposed to be The Crooked Nose of Nai," I said, pointing. "The one the Indians call Naikoon. This is where Seegay got wrecked."

"Who's Seegay?" asked Mary.

"He was a great Haida navigator. Twice he survived the waters of the strait. Once his canoe split. He clung to a floating gunbox with one hand and with the other he rescued the chief and held him till they drifted ashore. Chief Weah died, but Seegay was young, he survived. Then when he was middle-aged his boat was wrecked again, this time off the spit. Once more he made it to shore, but he was so weakened by exposure out on Rose Spit that he later succumbed."

We stood looking out onto the long nose of sand. The wind blew the last of the grasses flat.

"Look! Cape Ball," said Mary, turning to point south. "That's where we were two days ago." I winced at the thought of trying to connect our tracks. "Our eyes can do the walking," said Mary and relief washed over me.

We sat on the top of the highest dune. At the edge of the world to our right was Cape Ball, in front of us, Rose Spit, and to the left the warm wind seemed to waft the dust of the civilization we had left behind in the crowded campsite of Tow Hill.

I caught sight of a moving dot with a plume of dust behind it. We watched it come closer, as if we were reeling it in.

"Truck," said Mary. "It's like fishing and catching a truck."

The blue pickup stopped within fifty feet of the dune on which we sat. We were not seen.

From the tailgate dropped a mob of children and a village dog of many varieties. Out of the cab climbed a man and a woman. Black hair shone in the light. On the woman's head was a circular beaded band from which hung two white feathers. In her ears were two pieces of silver that flashed and tinkled when she leaned over the back of the pickup. She withdrew a darkly stained spruceroot basket. It looked old, rich with years of berry stain. Perhaps it was her grandmother's treasure. Out of it she pulled a stack of plastic honey tins with wire bails. Children flocked around her.

The hands of the newest generation reached for the honey tins. I realized there would be no weaving of baskets now that plastic had been invented.

The children fanned out between the dunes. It was late for wild strawberries. Mary and I sat and ate some of our Crispy Cakes and cheese. The family collected some small treasures that we hadn't noticed out of the sand, then on some hidden signal they drew together to dump the treasures into the spruceroot basket.

Returning from the truck with fish sandwiches, the children sat on their dune and ate their lunch. The small dog darted from place to place, picking up crumbs coated in sand.

At another hidden signal the family picked up their belongings, stacked the plastic pails and poured back into the truck. The dog jumped in last. With a scrunch of tires the pickup rolled back, swung wide onto the dunebuggy path, and with a shudder of dust it vanished down the trail with the stack of plastic pots rattling. No words had been said. Mary and I stared after them. "Ghosts," said Mary. The truck had become a mirage again.

"This is what the shifting sands cover and uncover," I ventured at last. "Savage Life on the Frontier, the history books would have called it. It's only the plastic that contemporizes them."

"Tow Hill isn't coming any closer," Mary sighed, as we turned back toward it. "The treadmill of North Beach. Perhaps the place is bewitched."

Thoughts of Indian spirits flashed through my mind: the giant Salmon; the mythical Tow, a spider monster of the landmark rock bluff; Nai, the evil spirit of Rose Spit. The soft rain of truth was sifting against my face. I squinted off into the distance, light-headed. There were two dragons moving in my peripheral vision. I blinked out the rain, blinked again. Had Mary seen them, too?

"Look," she said. "What are they?"

The hair was alive on the back of my neck. "Let's catch up," I said, "and find out."

We hurried toward them, coming to their tracks first. They were long, with toes, and with tail marks. "It's like the tracks of giant otters," Mary gasped. She poked her hiking pole into one of them.

In time we overtook the strange creatures.

"Hello!" we called.

When they saw us, the apparitions stopped, waited. We saw tails turn into kelp ropes of bleach bottles.

"We wondered, what . . . " I blustered, out of breath. "It looked so strange."

"We're doing it for the environment," the woman said, as she held up the piece of kelp with the bottles rattling. "We've done it on ten different beaches this year. We just gather stuff up and when the strings get too long we drag everything up into the bushes and pile it up out of sight of the beach. That way at least the beaches stay looking like the world beauty spots they could be."

"A plastic midden," I said.

"Yes. We clean up the mess humanity leaves behind. It's our summer project. We've been treating it as a game," she went on. "There's enough trash on this beach to keep us busy for days — the worst we've seen, and on one of the most

beautiful beaches. I don't know why people take such things
for granted."

"We could help, but I'm just too exhausted from hiking
to the spit," said Mary. I was in full agreement. Tow Hill
seemed as far away as ever.

Another surprise meal awaited us in camp. Fresh crab.
"We were given a bucketful at the Masset wharf," our
neighbours explained. "And we may just be noisy again
tonight, so we're making a peace offering early. We'll even
cook them for you."

Mary and I didn't confess that we were far too weary to hear
anything that night; we sat down to a glass of sweetwater wine
while the great chefs of Tow Hill went to work on our dinner.

Before turning in I religiously carried the bits to the sea.

"You know," said Mary suddenly, "we don't have to keep
all those agates."

I was relieved. I had been feeling quite guilty. "It's something
to do with throwing away fish remains, isn't it?" I asked.

"I can see in the future this beach may have no agates on it," said Mary.

There was no sleep of oblivion for me that night. I had overindulged in the rich food. I lay in bed with my eyes seeing Tow Hill and the endless beach; then sometime during the night the Plastic Bleach Bottle Spirit rose up before me to thank mankind for throwing such an abundance of plastic into the sea. In spite of my good deed with the agates, I ended the North Beach trek with a nightmare of the worst kind.

# 21.   Tour Bus

WE WOKE up to steady rain thrumming seriously on the tents, on the salal, on the hedge of high grass that sheltered us from the exposed beach. Out on the open shore the wind was driving the rain before it in sheets.

With grim lips we made a beeline to the camp cookshed, carrying Mary's stove and our breakfast wrapped in garbage bags.

Ten other campers with the same idea were already in the shed, while two diehards were down on the beach hunting for razor clams. Soon they, too, joined us, scattering a shower of water the way dogs do when they come out from a swim. There followed a lesson in how to catch razor clams.

"Look for a neck sticking out of the sand, then plunge the blade of your shovel in just behind, dig, and dig fast, then get down and scoop with your hands like crazy — get the thing out 'for it gets away 'cause them suckers can go like greased pigs — down their tunnels like rats."

We didn't go out to try it. The tide was coming in too fast for us to be tempted. Yesterday's hike to Rose Spit had given us a full taste of rain and sand.

We were just settling down to the warmth in the community cookshed. Mary was enjoying chatting with other campers as a contrast to our usual camping style, and I was

putting a hard line around a figure in a yellow slicker when
suddenly the interlude was interrupted. A large tour bus had
turned the bend in the road. With a rumble and a squeal of
airbrakes it pulled up beside the cookhouse. I watched,
dismayed and disheartened and aware suddenly of the loss of
a style of camping that I was used to. This was not the
wilderness, I thought, as forty pairs of eyes lined the beach
side of the bus windows, not the sort of sketching, camping,
tripping I had in mind . . . A loudspeaker blared out that there
would be a half-hour rest stop. Forty people pushed and
shoved their way into the cookshed. We were surrounded. I
thought of the figurative shovel. It had been thrust in behind
us; we were being scooped like crazy . . .

Tourists need to cram as much life as possible into their
few short minutes at a reststop or viewpoint. There was half an
hour for them of Agate Beach before they would be bussed
away. Out of the corner of my eye I saw two tourists bypass the
stampede into the shed and dash down onto the beach. They
returned twenty minutes later with handfuls of agates. Were
they some of mine? Mary's? We exchanged smiling glances.
The rest of the busload gathered round. The noise level in the

shed peaked the decibel range as questions poured forth without pause for response. After several moments, a certain quiet bunch of campers in their yellow oilskins scuttled away into the rain like a herd of disturbed crabs when the first foot stirs the water at the edge of a tide pool.

The rain, like the tourists, passed and was gone. We climbed Tow Hill, both of us mumbling that this sort of camping was not our style. Next time, we said, we would go hunting for wilderness.

Observing the world from five hundred feet above the beach where the cliff rises sharp and sheer from the shore gave us yet another perspective on the beauty of the magic islands of the Queen Charlottes.

"It seems to be an untapped treasure trove," I said. "An artist's paradise." Sudden sun broke the clouds and we stood looking down the precipice of bare basalt, we looked with the eyes of the North Beach eagles. Below us lay the long arc of shore and the white rollers crashing in endlessly upon resistant yet yielding sand. Matchstick trees, toothpick driftlogs and, behind the sand, a muskeg bog that stretched off as far as eye could see. There were no tourists there. The huge wild part of B.C., I knew in those moments, would keep me busy exploring for a lifetime.

Together we looked southward toward the Moresby Group, the wild, unpopulated lower islands of Haida Gwai. I yearned even harder for wild camps off by themselves. This vista from Tow Hill was only the outer halo of paradise.

# 22.  Mountain

DAMPENED DOWN by a rainfall in Prince Rupert, I set up my tent to dry under cottonwoods that clattered. I listened to the rattling bones of shamans of the past. From this place, the Bulkley and the Skeena rivers joined to plunge seaward. I had heard of the Grease Trail. At this river's mouth, in the early days, eulachon gathered; candlefish, they were called, because they were so oily they would burn if you set them alight. The fish eaters also gathered: gulls, eagles, seals and man. It became the gathering place, the centre of the world. Predators came to collect the fish by the million. Fermented, the oil became one of the greatest delicacies of the aboriginals' diet; everything was eaten in its bastings, and Native health was assured.

I walked downstream over the cobbles. I stood by the rushing water, inspired as the Indians must have been by its fecundity. By its gift of food, the eulachon. In this place two rivers rushed into each other's arms over lozenges of flat stones. The cataract turned the image of the high mountain above me, its crown hidden in snow and mist, to white foam. I sat down.

I painted the meeting of textures, the mist rolling down over the snow, absorbing the shadowed crags and drifting on. I swallowed a lump deep within. Tears came to my eyes.

How? How was I to capture this, how get my awe down on paper, how uncover what lay in the deepest layers of my heart? I sat with a blank white page. The world was beautiful no matter what happened to it, through anything that mankind might do. Nature looked out without reproach, and the invitation was always there. My pen was learning the shape of its own calligraphy — practise was the secret, and then, practise. Get out there and practise some more.

I watched the scene fade through ice blue to peach to rose to crimson and then fade away into the shadowy blue of evening.

At last I knew, as surely as I could know of my own humanity, that I would go on trying to capture the elusive moods of wilderness, no matter how ineptly my pen portrayed them, for the rest of my life. It had become vital to me, this drawing and painting, though I did not know the rhyme or reason, only that while I worked at my sketches I belonged to moments where time did not exist, that I dipped into the essence that was creator.

As I sat by the confluence of the rivers I looked out of a

shell that was human to the mountain going dark. There were no artificial lights anywhere, just a moon coming up over mountain crests to gild the snow with a pale light. I would stumble to camp over moonlit cobbles, knowing that I would find my way back even without the path.

I stood up. To the meeting of rivers, and to the mountain Guardian, and to the night moon, I silently called out, "Goodbye. I will be back, and perhaps I'll know how to sketch you better next time. Goodbye . . . "

# 23.   West Coast Thanksgiving

I CAME home to the work of being caretaker of my land in Deep Cove. I began to paint in the mornings, to hew wood and tend gardens in the afternoons. Mary had gone back to cultivating her vegetables and to the day-to-day challenge of her chosen work. We kept our contact and made plans for future trips.

I thoroughly enjoyed returning to the routines, but something always niggled in the back of my being — the restlessness to be out again. Each time I wheeled past the shed with a barrow of tools or trash, I caught sight of *Raven Moon*. She appeared to be sulking in the depths of my workshop as she hung airborne from her dusty nylon straps. Hiking by foot had consumed my travelling time for a couple of summers. Now winter was coming on, and I would soon be restricted to day trips and local travel. Thanksgiving would be the time to go, I decided; there was just time for one more paddle before winter.

I set my sights on Barkley Sound. It would take a week to get ready. I made false promises to spend extra time with my dogs and cats come winter; then I took the dogs hunting and foraging in the closest wild park every day until the house sitter arrived and promised to continue running the hounds in

the last big stand of trees in North Saanich, and to let my cats vie for lap priority.

I got out *Raven Moon*. As soon as she gained the truck roof racks, she looked puffed up and ready for travel on the seven seas. I threw my kit of art supplies and my boxes of camping gear into the truck. I put her in reverse and cleared the driveway.

Toquart Bay was merely a stopping place for sleep, and then I was out with *Raven Moon* loaded to the gunwales. Her toggles began to sing contentedly as they always do in the waters of Barkley Sound, which has become her adopted paradise. It has been too long, she seemed to say. I thought of her excursions as never being quite as challenging as those of the intrepid group that paddled their Nordkapps around the Horn. In fact, what I did might have seemed like tame Sunday afternoon paddles along the Gorge to some, but to me they brought enough excitement and challenge to pique my interest for a lifetime.

I set the bow in the direction of Turret Island and passed off the tip of Hand, the Brabants, Willis and Turtle. At Willis Island the tide, which had once all but swept me past before I could slip between the rocks into the gap, peaked the waves off the rockpile into three-foot arrow points. I swung wide and carried on, facing the wind so that my eyes streamed and the water came over the foredeck and washed me down in an icy bath. I was full of spirit for one more trip before the winter, and next year? Who knows? Perhaps *Raven Moon* would seek the waters of the uninhabited part of the Queen Charlottes.

I slipped through the channel and came facing in through wild water to the camping spot on the Turret Island midden. I rode up high onto the beach in a swath of wave and jumped out. I was glad to be back; it had seemed forever! The places I touched down were treasures I wanted to visit and revisit until I or my kayak cracked asunder. Each new one became one more in the collection to return to. Where would it end?

Barkley Sound, the Queen Charlottes, Nootka Island . . . all of the coastal islands of British Columbia had been supplying me amply with light — and here I was out harvesting. My journals were growing yearly. In the winter I would relive all the summer and make plans for next year and the next. I saw a wall of years stretching out like a great roll call. Where would it end? The paintings and drawings were only the reflections of being there. I was the lucky one — I could live it, I could do it.

I landed on the familiar beach with such great exuberance that I frightened away an eagle who was enjoying his repast hidden in the rocks. He hurried skywards. As he rose he dropped his gleaming silver prize and didn't return to retrieve it. I watched the raptor soar higher and higher in ever widening circles. I stood holding the fish and watching the sky. It was another omen, but what did it mean?

In the hold, safely packed in the waterproof zippered bag I had made the previous winter, was my logbook and my sketchbook, with a set of new pencils and pens. It was all I needed, really, the tools for an artist's harvesting. I got out the sketchbook, now scratched and marked by many travels. I began to sketch the sky of eagles.

At last I was compelled to return to the mundane. I cleaned the salmon as contentment with my new location

surrounded me. I began to recall some of the experiences of
the last few years. Nissen Bight and Rose Spit. I couldn't have
painted them if I had not gone there to experience them first-
hand. I had needed to feel under a century of undisturbed
sand that fine sharpness of the halibut lure and to make
contact with the people of an age now gone. I had needed to
know the wolves were there, still roaming in the living wild,
and to hear the voice of the crazy woman, goading me to yet

greater effort. I had needed the blistered feet of Rose Spit, and the hunger of Cape Ball. They taught me empathy for the harshness of life in the sands. All had been lessons in the shaping of my life as an artist. All places had been my learning ground — and there was more yet to come, I knew, as much as I could squeeze in.

Like *Raven Moon,* I was now welcoming the strange, dark current midstream, knowing that somewhere in a past I barely understood I had chosen to push out from shore. The light of the British Columbia coast had lured me. The eye of a being that stretched through the ages, saw the light for harvesting, and offered it, shining down the tides in that direction.

Surrounding me was the sound of water. I heard flute music and upon investigating found that a few previous days of fresh rain had filled the Turret Island sipwell until it trickled with a crystal clear sound. I went for the lid of my thermos and dipped out a portion.

In half an hour my tent was up and the afternoon wind was sighing down to a faint warm breath. I got the fire on and prepared a pan for the fish. At last I stood up by my fire to make a special toast: "To the tides of life," I said to my audience of dark hemlock trees. "Some of us drift out from the back eddies, out into the current to fulfil our purpose in some unique way, to partake of the world, of life, to its fullest measure."

I held up the thermos lid, now a crystal goblet, and the water, now the purest wine. "To the harvest." I drank the libation and sat down to my Thanksgiving dinner.

Perhaps tomorrow I would get out to Clarke Island, and on to Dicebox . . . Overhead wheeled the eagle, caught by a net of small, moving, shadowy clouds that turned him as dark as he was light against the blue sky.

Omens, I thought — more omens . . .

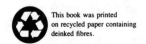

This book was printed
on recycled paper containing
deinked fibres.

Printed in Canada